JOHN G. PATON

Missionary to the Cannibals
of the South Seas

Paul Schlehlein

THE BANNER OF TRUTH TRUST

THE BANNER OF TRUTH TRUST
3 Murrayfield Road, Edinburgh EH12 6EL, UK
PO Box 621, Carlisle, PA 17013, USA

ISBN
Print: 978 1 84871 765 7
EPUB: 978 1 84871 766 4
Kindle: 978 1 84871 767 1

Typeset in 11/15 pt Adobe Garamond Pro at
The Banner of Truth Trust, Edinburgh

Printed in the USA by
Versa Press, Inc.,
East Peoria, IL.

To Lindy,

of course

'murandziwa wa nga i wa mina'
(Tinsimu 6:3)

'I am grateful to Paul Schlehlein for providing a new look at the life and ministry of John G. Paton. Early in my life I was enduringly impacted by Paton's autobiography edited by his brother, James. The story was a stunning account of dedication, desperation, sacrifice at the most extreme level, and selfless love to Christ. I was marked for life by the amazing missionary adventure and the far-reaching and lasting gospel impact of that one man empowered and protected by the Holy Spirit. In this age when giving a trophy to everyone is standard, and when minimal Christian dedication is celebrated, all believers need to go back to the past to see what true devotion to Christ and the gospel really looks like. You will see it in John Paton.'

JOHN MACARTHUR

Contents

Illustrations

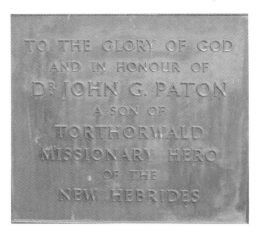

TO THE GLORY OF GOD
AND IN HONOUR OF
Dʳ JOHN G. PATON
A SON OF
TORTHORWALD
MISSIONARY HERO
OF THE
NEW HEBRIDES

Dʳ JOHN G. PATON
1824 – 1907

"AND OTHER SHEEP I HAVE, WHICH
ARE NOT OF THIS FOLD: THEM
ALSO I MUST BRING, AND THEY
SHALL HEAR MY VOICE: AND THERE
SHALL BE ONE FLOCK, AND ONE
SHEPHERD."

JOHN 10:16

*Brass memorials of John G. Paton on the gate pillars of
Torthorwald Kirk, Dumfriesshire, Scotland.*

Acknowledgements

M ANY friends were involved in the creation of this book. Matt Sawa sent across the Atlantic the initial, difficult-to-find books that got the project underway. Prof. Koos Van Rooy and his wife, Regina, opened their lovely home in the Soutpansberg Mountains so that I could carve out the initial structure of the book. Pastor Tim Leaman, a model of faithful pastor and student of the word, provided valuable insights as well. My wife, Melinda, with vim and grace, helped carry every phase of the project to fruition.

I would also like to thank Drs John MacArthur and Steven Lawson for their kind and generous commendations of this book.

Paul Schlehlein
Mbhokota Village,
South Africa
September 18, 2017

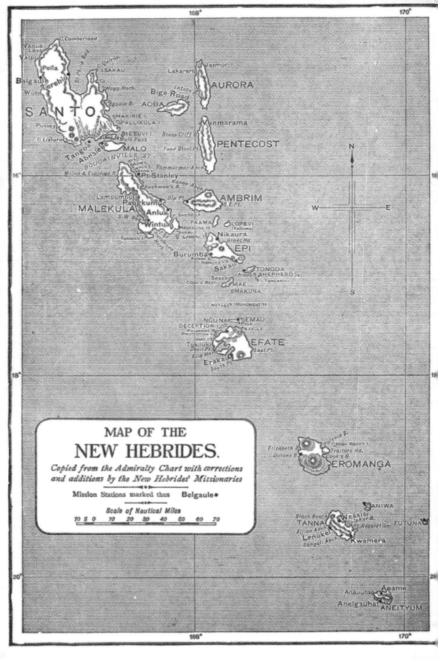

MAP OF THE
NEW HEBRIDES.

*Copied from the Admiralty Chart with corrections
and additions by the New Hebrides' Missionaries*

Mission Stations marked thus   Belgaule •

Scale of Nautical Miles

10 5 0   10   20   30   40   50   60   70

INTRODUCTION

The Haunts of Savagery

J UNE 25, 2009, was the day I learned God had not made me a seaman.

As the whitecaps smacked the keel of our boat, my eye surveyed nothing but open sea. We were sailing for the island of Anjouan, one of three tiny atolls making up the Comoros archipelago. The distance from one island to the other was just two millimetres on the globe, but the trip lasted nine hours. At the time, several mission organizations considered the natives on Anjouan among the most unreached peoples in the world. Isolation from the gospel and persecution for the gospel had led to opposition to the gospel.

Leaving my wife and newborn behind temporarily, I had hoped my previous studies of Bantu languages would help make inroads among this isolated, volcanic group largely untouched by the gospel. Ibrahim, the passenger to my left, became our teacher for the turbulent voyage. With each passing hour, as my dexterity in the language increased, so did the number of passengers discharging their seasickness overboard. Still fresh upon me now are the feelings of fear, the prospects of hope, the clouds of doubt, and the absence of regret.

My experiences there have caused me to become unusually knit to John Paton, for it was nearly 150 years earlier that he found himself in a scenario resembling my own. He sailed upon another ocean, in a different time, to a more hazardous place, and yet as he and his new wife peered over the prow of their ship, beyond the wasteland of graybeards and into the midst of the islands, I surmise he experienced similar feelings. I wonder if the author who attempts to capture the ethos of such a great missionary—all the while feeling his own immeasurable shortcomings—should not in some way emit the aroma coming from the same dusty paths, the same paralyzing fear, and the same pernicious surroundings.

This is the story of an island of cannibals, their journey out of darkness, and the man who led them to the light. It is a story that begins with heads slung in shame, only to be raised in joy before the Lamb who bore their disgrace.

Such indignity and humiliation came from, among other things, their proclivity for the abominable act of cannibalism. But just as stars shine brightest in a moonless sky, so the grace of the Lord Jesus flashes most brilliantly before the man-eaters of the New Hebrides, as this retelling of a South Seas missionary shows:

> 'Isaia, have you yourself ever tasted human flesh?' The eyes seek the ground, and the mottled foot for a minute or two

toys with the grass. Without raising his eyes he touches his lips with his finger. It is enough. He has eaten and is ashamed. ... At last, the old, uncomely face is raised again, and on it there is an expression of sadness, tempered with nascent joy. It is far more beautiful, that face, than the traveller had judged at first. 'It is true, sir, I have eaten. I am full of shame. But, sir, it was in the days of darkness before the light ... came to Fiji. God is good-hearted and I am forgiven.'[1]

Missionaries like Paton need to be heard afresh. Our slumbering congregations devoid of zeal and passion need heroes with his kind of evangelistic pluck. Paton was an icon in his day—a household name in Great Britain and Australia. Contemporaries such as C. H. Spurgeon called him the 'King of the Cannibals'.

Paton's *Autobiography*, his wife's *Letters and Sketches*, and his son's *Later Years and Farewell* serve as the three primary sources for this biography. George Patterson's biography of Geddie, *Missionary Life among the Cannibals* and Peter Barnes's monograph on Aneityum are key resources as well. The *Autobiography* provides the core structure, covering the whole of Paton's life save the final ten years. If the *Autobiography* is in fast-paced, black and white, Margaret Paton's *Sketches* comes in high-definition colour. She provides the details of

[1] John Burton, *The Fiji of Today* (London: C. H. Kelly, 1910), pp. 150-51.

daily life her husband was often loathe to give. *Later Years and Farewell* calls Paton's *Autobiography* a 'missionary classic' and 'complete'. 'It cannot be excelled', they say. But it was last revised in 1897, meaning ten years of the great missionary's life still remained. Thus, in 1910, his son Frank and a dear friend A. K. Langridge published an account covering the last portion of Paton's life. James Paton, John's youngest brother and editor of his *Autobiography*, believed he would one day write a biography of his brother, but death claimed him just three weeks before John's passing. Thus, for over one hundred years, the life of one of history's greatest missionaries has stood mostly untouched.[2] The fertile field lay fallow, a treasure hidden beneath a century of unknowing generations.

The goals for this book are fourfold. First, I would like to infuse in the reader the kind of unflappable courage and indefatigable moxie for which Paton was known. In our world of diplomacy and emotional sensitivity, the South Seas missionary comes with bare-knuckled bravery. We need men like Paton to put steel in our spines, love in our hearts, and assurance in our minds that there are times to double the shot and shorten the fuse.

Second, my hope is that the ink of Paton's pen will arrest today's audience as it did the public a century ago. This book quotes Paton in abundance. This is by design, for not only is Paton clear and vivid, but he owns that elusive knack for the well-turned phrase. His unyielding courage gives wings

---

[2] One exception is the summary of Paton's *Autobiography*: Jim Cromarty, *King of the Cannibals* (Darlington: Evangelical Press, 1998).

to his words. Not many can write and inspire like the mighty Scotsman, as the following quote testifies: 'I knew not, for one brief hour, when or how attack [against my life] might be made; and yet, with my trembling hand clasped in the hand once nailed on Calvary, and now swaying the sceptre of the universe, calmness and peace and resignation abode in my soul.'[3]

Third, my desire is that this exploration of Paton's life would encourage the faint-hearted and lift up the hands which hang down. Over a century ago, his *Autobiography* gave hope to worn-out, discouraged missionaries in obscure places when they saw what God had done among the cannibals of the South Seas.

Finally, I wish to pull out compelling lessons from his ministry in the chapters that follow his biography. Chapter five describes Paton's accent on family. Chapter six looks at Paton's philosophy of calling. The Patons believed *all* Christians are called to tell others of Christ; his son refusing to blunt the edge of duty for the Western world wrote: 'We argue, fearlessly, that what has been done in the haunts of savagery can be done in the slums of civilization.'[4] Chapter seven focuses on Paton's most enduring quality—courage. What else but unbridled daring could move someone to leave a successful ministry at home and cross an ocean to an isolated people still living in the Stone Age? When the Lord sought for a man

[3] John G. Paton, *The Autobiography of the Pioneer Missionary to the New Hebrides (Vanuatu)* (1898; repr. Edinburgh: Banner of Truth Trust, 2016), p. 117.

[4] Frank Paton, *Lomai of Lenakel: A Hero of the New Hebrides* (London: Hodder and Stoughton, 1903), p. vi.

to build up the wall among the cannibals and stand in the breach of heathenism, he found John Paton. Chapter eight gives the reader a view of Paton's theology of risk by analyzing his deft capacity to merge caution and danger. This section investigates how a life so consecrated to Jesus could, like a ship ballasted with iron, ride out the worst of gales. Chapter nine addresses the various issues surrounding Paton's strategies in giving the gospel to a remote land, while chapter ten examines one of his greatest gifts—unrelenting evangelism.

J. Graham Miller, himself a missionary to the New Hebrides, salutes the gospel ground-breakers that were not alive long enough to savour the fruit.

> I was now clear as to my duty to provide the New Hebrides Church with the record of God's work in the planting of his Church there. I calculated that the blood of more than one hundred martyrs and missionary pioneers had been shed to bring our Church into being. They were brown missionaries from Polynesia; black missionaries from Aneityum, Efate and Nguna; and white missionaries from Canada, England, and Scotland. Where they laid down their lives in loneliness and apparent failure there is today a living Church comprising more than half the population of the New Hebrides.[5]

[5] J. Graham Miller, *A Day's March Nearer Home* (Edinburgh: Banner of Truth Trust, 2010), p. 201.

Happy was John Paton, missionary pioneer, to lay down his life in 'loneliness and apparent failure'. For years he sowed terrain that stole away his family, his health, and his most vibrant years, only in God's grace to reap a harvest that would take decades to mature and an eternity to enjoy. The sower and the reaper may rejoice together Jesus said (John 4:36); the life of Paton is an invitation to delight in both.

PART ONE

PATON'S LIFE

Torthorwald Kirk.

1

The Early Years

God gave his best, his Son, to me; and I give back
my best, my all, to him.[1]

—John G. Paton

O N August 30, 1858, four months after its departure
from bonnie Scotland, John Paton's ship dropped
anchor off the coast of a sandy island in the sprawling Pacific.
Overcome with excitement, Paton and his nineteen-year old
wife transferred their cargo on to a small, overloaded boat
and perched themselves among the boxes. As they shoved off,
the mainmast broke, nearly decapitating Paton's new bride.
Though the vessel was now disabled and ten miles from shore,
the captain of the mother ship cruelly pulled away and left
them to their fate.

Under the rays of the sweltering sun, the missionaries and
natives struggled for hours to bring their two boats ashore.
The wind was against them. Paton could not swim. But this
was not the worst of it. 'We drifted steadily in the direction

[1] Paton, *Autobiography*, p. 444.

of Tanna, an island of cannibals, where our goods would have been plundered and all of us cooked and eaten.'[2]

Thus began the missionary career of John G. Paton. These unpromising events were not only a harbinger of trials ahead, but were the opening lines of one of the greatest missionary stories ever told.

A noble heritage

Mission must look back before it marches forward. Like God's ark, the missionary enterprise is carried on the shoulders of consecrated men.

This may indicate why a country like Scotland—smaller in size than South Carolina—could produce such an array of missionaries in the nineteenth century. Alexander Somerville observed: 'Scotland, small as she is, has already told on the destinies of the world.'[3] Within a hundred years, she sent out missionaries such as Alexander Duff (India), David Livingstone (Africa), William Chalmers Burns (China), Robert Moffat (South Africa), Mary Slessor (Nigeria), Robert Morrison (China), Eric Liddell (China), and hundreds of others history, not heaven, has forgotten. They were sent and supported by church leaders such as Thomas Chalmers, Andrew and Horatius Bonar, Robert and James Haldane, and Robert Murray M'Cheyne. John Paton did not leave Scotland unescorted but followed in a long line of godly men.

[2] *Ibid.*, p. 64.
[3] Quoted, Iain H. Murray, *The Puritan Hope: A Study in Revival and the Interpretation of Prophecy* (London: Banner of Truth Trust, 1971), p. 158.

Ironically at the dawn of the nineteenth century, *rigor mortis* had settled upon the majority of Scottish pulpits. In vogue at the time was a form of liberalism, whose supple creed is well summarized by Jonathan's armour bearer: 'Do all that is in your heart' (1 Sam. 14:7). For them, Scripture was not an anchor to be fixed and planted but a sentiment to be cut and pasted—polished for a softer feel. But not everyone was dogmatically indefinite about theological convictions. Some men really believed what the Bible said.

God's Spirit began to work. Non-denominational missionary societies began springing up all over Scotland as evangelistic preaching penetrated the country. Thomas Chalmers exchanged his large congregation for the classroom, stirring great enthusiasm in the slumbering school at St Andrews. In 1824, to the dismay of the faculty, the Student Missionary Society was formed. Among the student members were Alexander Duff and the famed St Andrews Seven.[4]

[4] The era of the St Andrews Seven came on the heels of several revolutionary missionary advancements. When the six students first enrolled at St Andrews in 1822, they were nearly three decades removed from 1793 when the 'Father of Modern Missions', William Carey, set sail for India. Carey had bucked the norm by joining a new missionary society, assailing caste-laden India, and using his linguistic genius to eventually translate the Bible into forty-four languages and dialects. In 1807, the British Parliament voted to abolish the slave trade, largely through the efforts of William Wilberforce. Then in 1812, Adoniram Judson—after coming to Baptist convictions on his voyage to Calcutta—chose to minister independently in Burma until an American Baptist missions board finally chose to support him. Moreover, Carey's treatise, *An Inquiry into the Obligation of Christians to Use Means for the Conversion of the Heathens*, challenged traditional thinking about missions and launched the modern missionary movement. The St Andrews Seven now had several examples to show this was permissible and even wise to do.

Elsewhere Robert Haldane sold his estate and gave £25,000 to missions, an almost incalculable sum at the time. By 1825, over sixty local mission societies had been formed, including the Edinburgh and Glasgow Missionary Societies.

Home life became vibrant again, making the soil soft for evangelistic zeal. Fathers reclaimed their role as family prophet and became the first teachers of their children—laying unshakable foundations for their spiritual lives. One can catch a glimpse of this in Paton's boyhood home: 'As we rose from our knees, I used to look at the light on my father's face, and wish I were like him in spirit—hoping that, in answer to his prayers, I might be privileged and prepared to carry the blessed gospel to some portion of the heathen world.'[5]

While every godly home in Scotland may not have shared the same zeal for missions, most families agreed that if the father spurns his duties at home, he should not be surprised when Hophni and Phineas disdain the gospel. Homes full of spiritual life will invigorate the church.

All of this was happening amidst a renewed trust in the Scriptures. It was *the word* that now gave the impetus to go and to give. This is evident years later when metal gates in memory of John Paton were erected at the entrance of Torthorwald churchyard bearing the text: 'Other sheep I have which are not of this fold; them also I must bring' (John 10:16).[6] The same words can be found upon the gravestone of David Livingstone

[5] Paton, *Autobiography*, p. 21.

[6] Iain H. Murray, *A Scottish Christian Heritage* (Edinburgh: Banner of Truth Trust, 2006), p. 223.

in Westminster Abbey. This was a generation of biblical dependents, an era of scriptural fixation. It should not be surprising, then—amidst this whirlwind of spiritual activity—that hot and cold parishioners sitting side by side in the pews could no longer coexist. The Disruption of the Church of Scotland in 1843 was inevitable. Iain Murray writes:

> When the rising tide of evangelical conviction could endure no longer the interference of patrons over the scriptural right of congregations to elect their own ministers ... 451 ministers seceded to form the Free Church of Scotland, with Thomas Chalmers as the first Moderator. ... For the next several decades, there can be little question that this body became the most mission-minded denomination in Britain.[7]

It was within *this* milieu that John Paton arrived.

Early life

Born on May 24, 1824, near Dumfries in south-west Scotland, John Paton was the eldest of eleven children of James and Janet Paton. To put into perspective Paton's birth within the great century of missions, Adoniram Judson was falsely imprisoned as a spy in Burma two weeks later on June 8. Exactly six years after Paton's birth Alexander Duff landed in India, becoming the first overseas missionary from the Church of Scotland. William Carey, the father of modern missions, died ten years later on June 9, 1834.

---

[7] Murray, *Puritan Hope*, p. 169.

John wrote often of the Covenanter blood running through his veins and of those forebears who suffered for Christ's crown. Among his ancestors may have been Captain John Paton, one of the Scots Worthies who 'lived a hero and died a martyr'.[8] His father was a weaver who struggled to support his five sons and six daughters by producing woollen socks in their small cottage. Whatever the home lacked in earthly goods, however, James Paton made amends for in spiritual care. John spoke of his parents in the most reverential terms all his life. He almost worshipped the memory of his mother, calling her a 'bright-hearted, high-spirited, patient-toiling, and altogether heroic little woman'. He dedicated the opening chapters of his *Autobiography* to the honour of his parents, crediting them for all of his spiritual and ministerial success:

> Religion was presented to us with a great deal of intellectual freshness … it did not repel us, but kindled our spiritual interest. The talks which we heard were, however, genuine; not the make-believe of religious conversation, but the sincere outcome of their own personalities. That, perhaps, makes all the difference betwixt talk that attracts and talk that drives away.[9]

The Patons were members of the Reformed Presbyterian Church, which the elder Paton believed most clearly represented the church of the first and second Reformation in

[8] John Howie, *The Scots Worthies* (1870; repr. Edinburgh: Banner of Truth Trust, 2001), p. 494.

[9] Paton, *Autobiography*, p. 16.

Scotland. Circumstances disallowed the patriarch from entering the ministry in his youth but he vowed if God gave him sons, he would consecrate them unreservedly to the Lord's ministry. The Lord answered that prayer by supplying him with five sons, three of whom became ministers.

The family walked four miles to church every Sunday, though Mrs Paton rarely accompanied them due to frail health. 'Each of us, from very early days, considered it no penalty, but a great joy, to go with our father to the church; the four miles were a treat to our young spirits.' Upon their return, Paton's father would pace the living-room floor, recounting to mother each detail of the sermon and inviting his children to interject. Such a scene recalls Deuteronomy 6:7: 'You shall teach [the Scriptures] diligently to you children, and shall talk of them when you sit in your house, and when you walk by the way.' John's father was also steadfast in leading the family in morning and evening prayer, Bible-reading, catechism, and singing. If this family worship had been mere homework, or simply a task to check off, the Paton children would have rebelled against such hypocrisy. Instead, it was sincere and authentic.

> None of us can remember that any day ever passed unhallowed thus; no hurry for market, no rush to business, no arrival of friends or guests, no trouble or sorrow, no joy or excitement, ever prevented at least our kneeling around the family altar, while the High Priest led our prayers to God and offered himself and his children there.[10]

[10] *Ibid.*, p. 14.

In his early years Paton attended school where Bible and catechism were taught as ardently as mathematics and grammar. Before the age of twelve he was expected to work the stocking frames with this father from six in the morning till ten at night, with half-hour breaks for meals. In his free time he laboured over his books, especially the classical languages, for already as a young boy he was unusually focused on the serious matters of the Lord's work and had determined to be a gospel missionary. While other boys his age rested, played football, and dabbled in other games, he was poring over his books.

Missionary service was no boyish dream. When a government official guaranteed him a promotion and special training if he would simply sign a seven-year contract, Paton refused. The agent was irate: 'Will you refuse an offer that many gentlemen's sons would be proud of?' Paton replied: 'My life is given to another Master … to the Lord Jesus; and I want to prepare as soon as possible for his service in the proclaiming of the gospel.'

God in his providence honoured such faithfulness. Paton soon found a position as a tract distributor for a congregation in Glasgow, a post he obtained by writing two lengthy poems on the Scottish Covenanters. Though the pay was meagre, it came with one year of seminary training that greatly aided his ambition to learn. Though the long hours and lack of good food were a heavy weight upon him, it was his constant lack of finances that forced him to drop out of school periodically.

Low Green Street, Calton, Glasgow in 1868,
part of the district assigned to Paton as a City Missioner.

But even while he wandered the streets looking for work, his father's God was guiding him. He found a day job in a tough area of Glasgow teaching school to young people, and in the evenings he taught older students who had just finished their day's work at the mills and coal mines.

Thereafter, for the next ten years, he worked tirelessly as one of the evangelists for the Glasgow City Mission. Besides spending four hours a day visiting house to house, his schedule was filled with gospel tasks nearly every evening. On Mondays he ran a Bible study. On Wednesdays he held a prayer meeting, usually composed of half the Sunday attendance, whereby he would expound a Scripture text and apply it. Thursdays saw him catechising the new members' class. On Fridays he led a singing class to prepare for Sunday worship. On Saturdays he ran a Total Abstinence Class in which young people were taught to 'fear the very name of intoxicating drink, and to hate and keep far away from everything that led to intemperance'. He would preach to his beloved poor and often ragged flock of souls in any place he could find, including haylofts and the open air. It was here within the cobbled streets of Glasgow that Paton's pastor's heart was forged. He tasted the joys of seeing drunks, who 'could not pray', turn from their sins and believe. He felt the sting, too, of the hardened heart. As Paton sat beside a man on his deathbed, the dying man hoisted his fist to God, exclaiming: 'I believe there is a devil, and a God, and a just God, too; but I have hated him in life, and I hate him in death!' Paton saw that men love darkness rather than light in *every* culture.

At six o'clock each Sunday morning he would run from house to house arousing spiritual infants for his Bible class. Five to six hundred people began attending his weekly sermons. Soon his ministry was seen to be among the most successful the City Mission had ever known. But he never forgot his dream of world missions; the flame of cross-cultural evangelism still burned hot in his soul. His single purpose in Glasgow, he wrote, was to become 'qualified as a preacher of the gospel of Christ, to be owned and used by him for the salvation of perishing men'.

From 1847 to 1856 he would attend the University of Glasgow, the Reformed Presbyterian Divinity Hall, and medical classes at the local college.

When the Roman Catholics began bullying his flock and sending death threats to coerce him to leave, Paton displayed the indefatigable moxie that would characterize the rest of his ministry. He refused to cower to their demands. 'Let them see that bullying makes you afraid, and they will brutally and cruelly misuse you; but defy them fearlessly, or take them by the nose, and they will crouch like whelps beneath your feet.'

The early foundations of John Geddie

Though prior missionaries had done some preliminary work on the islands, John Geddie was undoubtedly the first to set down roots and is therefore considered the founder of the mission on the New Hebrides. A brief survey of Geddie's life and ministry will help keep John Paton's work in focus.

Geddie was born in Scotland on April 10, 1815, and emigrated with his family the next year to Nova Scotia. Interested in missions as a youth and converted in his teens, he was licensed to preach by the Presbytery of Pictou at the age of twenty-two and married Charlotte MacDonald the following year. She would bear him eight children. As a young minister he founded a missionary society in his congregation and convinced the small group of Presbyterian churches in Nova Scotia to engage in a foreign mission of her own—even though the church's own ministers were often ill supported. Many believe Geddie's most important contribution to the church of Christ was the initial idea and formulation of Canadian churches to support a foreign mission work.

When the London Missionary Society temporarily suspended sending missionaries to the western Polynesian islands of the New Hebrides due to the dangers surrounding John Williams' death, the Presbyterian churches of Nova Scotia jumped at the chance to fill the gap. Geddie quickly volunteered.

Not surprisingly, some in the church urged him to stay, arguing he was entirely unfit for the work because of his 'weak bodily presence'—apparently forgetting that the great missionary to the Gentiles was considered 'weak, and his speech of no account' (2 Cor. 10:10). Geddie was indeed shy, small and boyish-looking, but his gifts made him admirably qualified for the work.[11]

On November 3, 1846, John and Charlotte Geddie with their two small children left Halifax, Nova Scotia for the South Seas. A month earlier he had written a farewell letter to his congregation.

> I have anticipated a voyage of 18,000 miles over the mighty ocean, through many latitudes and divers climes; but there

[11] Others argued there were not enough labourers at home. Geddie answered: 'Whatever our wants at home, we will not suffer by doing good to others. It is when churches endeavour to become a blessing to others that they are usually blessed themselves.' George Patterson, *Missionary Life Among the Cannibals: Being the Life of the Rev. John Geddie, D.D., First Missionary to the New Hebrides* (Toronto: James Campbell & Son, James Bain & Son, and Hart & Co., 1882), p. 49.

is One who 'ruleth the raging of the sea, and stilleth the waves thereof when they arise'; and there is safety under his watchful care. I have looked forward to the time when I must forego the blessings of civilization, the comforts of social life, and the sweets of home, and expose myself to the inveterate prejudice, the repulsive arrogance, and the deep-rooted superstition of a barbarous people.[12]

After eight months of language study in Samoa, the Geddies moved in July 1848 to Aneityum, an island of 4,000 people, 35 miles southeast of Tanna. They considered it the least dangerous island of the group, though they would face their share of trials. Nevertheless, speaking of Aneityum, Geddie confesses, 'On no occasion have we seen or heard anything to awaken our fears as to our personal safety. In this we are privileged above our brethren who were formerly stationed on Tanna.'[13]

For a decade various forms of mission work had existed on the islands but never in permanent form. John Williams dropped three Samoan teachers in Tanna on November 19, 1839, before being killed on Erromanga just days later. Some time afterwards, LMS missionaries George Turner and Henry Nisbet came to Tanna in the New Hebrides but by January of 1843 they were gone. Native teachers came and went. Turner and A. W. Murray returned in 1845 to Aneityum but did not remain. Though conversions on the islands were few, the irregular Christian presence was softening the soil.

<hr>

[12] Patterson, *Missionary Life Among the Cannibals* p. 61.
[13] *Ibid.*, p. 184.

The Geddies were determined to stay. They printed books, treated diseases, and started schools. By the end of the second year there were ten people attending their services. John Inglis and his wife Jessie arrived in Aneityum in 1852, six years prior to Paton. Though older and more cautious than Geddie and perhaps disadvantaged in learning the language, Inglis thrived. The years that followed were ones of immense fruit. The missionaries reduced the language to writing, translated the New Testament into Aneityumese, established dozens of schools, built two church buildings and witnessed over three hundred becoming church members. 'How rare it is for the first missionaries to any race to see such results from their efforts in the same time, even where there was a band of missionaries employed! And how few ministers in the home field are permitted to see such fruit of their labours!'[14]

After fifteen years in Aneityum, the Geddies returned to Nova Scotia to tell the stirring accounts of God's work in the New Hebrides. They returned to the islands in 1866, but Geddie's health was poor. He died on December 14, 1872. The natives placed a placard in his honour behind a church pulpit in Aneityum. It read, in part: 'In memory of John Geddie, D.D., born in Scotland 1815 ... Missionary sent from Nova Scotia to Aneityum for twenty-four years. When he landed

[14] Geddie faced his greatest trial in 1849 when he learned his colleague from Nova Scotia, Isaac Archibald, had seduced and committed adultery with a native woman. Geddie agreed to keep the matter quiet from the home board if Archibald would agree to resign. Though his motives were pure, it was a disastrous mistake by Geddie. The matter over the following years would bring him emotional strain and heartache, much of which could have been avoided had he been forthright from the beginning.

in 1848, there were no Christians here, and when he left in 1872 there were no heathen.'

But interest on 'the dark island of Tanna' (as Geddie called it) began to grow—with the natives there desiring their own missionary. Such was the state of matters in the years before Paton arrived. While God was working on one side of the globe preparing the island of Tanna for gospel advancement, on the other side he was arranging Paton's steps to leave Scotland.

Call to the New Hebrides

Paton, now in his early thirties and his education complete, concluded the time was ripe to volunteer for service to the South Sea cannibals:

> I saw them perishing for lack of the knowledge of the true God and his Son Jesus, while my Green Street people had the open Bible and all the means of grace within easy reach, which, if they rejected, they did so wilfully, and at their own peril.[15]

In the beginning Paton told no one of his growing zeal to go. 'Without revealing the state of my mind to any person, this was the supreme subject of my daily meditation and prayer.' When he finally disclosed his plans to the Board, the Director of Missions broke out in tears of joy. Then, after confiding to his roommate that he had offered himself as a missionary to the New Hebrides ('I have been away signing my banishment'),

[15] *Ibid.*, p. 53.

Joseph Copeland replied: 'If they will accept of me, I am also resolved to go!' But any hopes Paton had for unfettered support among God's people soon vanished. In unison, pastors and parishioners alike offered a number of arguments against such a foolhardy task. Let the reader here take note: the criticisms the church gave sounded 'spiritual' in every way. One can even assume they attached a slew of proof texts in support.

At first Paton was urged to stay because of his gifting. After all, his Glasgow mission was enormously successful. Wouldn't life among the cannibals be a waste of his time and talents? The opposite tactic was used with John Geddie, with one venerated father of the congregation saying that he 'did not know a more unsuitable person than Mr. G.; that except zeal, which was the lowest of all, he did not possess one qualification for the work.'[16] The church reminded Paton that the sheep he had laboured to bring into the fold would most certainly scatter and fall away after his departure. Wasn't it *Jesus* who had compassion on sheep without a shepherd? This was followed by promises of money, the church offering to increase his pay to 'any reasonable salary' for which he cared to ask, just so long as he would remain at home.

When none of these arguments swayed him, they argued for the needs at home. They reasoned it would be better to evangelize first their neighbours and family members.[17] That

---

[16] Patterson, *Missionary Life Among the Cannibals*, p. 55.

[17] A similar mentality was already evident in Scotland at the end of the previous century. 'When the General Assembly of 1796 declined to take action to promote the aggressive evangelisation of the world, one of the arguments put forward to

most of the locals were not even doing *this* seemed to make little difference to them. Finally, they begged him to stay due to the prospects of danger and death. The famous missionary John Williams had been killed and eaten less than two decades earlier, the tragedy still fresh on everyone's minds. One dear Christian saint cried: 'The cannibals, you will be eaten by the cannibals!' To this, Paton replied:

> Mr Dickson, you are advanced in years now, and your own prospect is soon to be laid in the grave, there to be eaten by worms; I confess to you, that if I can but live and die serving and honouring the Lord Jesus, it will make no difference to me whether I am eaten by cannibals or by worms; and in the Great Day my resurrection body will arise as fair as yours in the likeness of our risen Redeemer.[18]

Paton was licensed as a preacher on December 1, 1857. He and Joseph Copeland then spent the next four months in Scottish churches asking for prayer and support. On March 23, 1858, in the church where he served as an elder, Paton was ordained as a minister and missionary to the southern New Hebrides. Meanwhile, John's younger brother Walter quit a successful job in order to take over the work at the Glasgow

justify such a policy of inaction was that there was quite enough for the church to do about its own doors. It was indeed quite true that there was already a problem of home heathenism. The lapsing of the masses had begun. Those, however, who pleaded this as a reason for doing nothing to spread the gospel to the regions beyond hardly thought that they would be so soon taken at their word and that inroads were to be made on the outfield of lapsed Christianity in Scotland.' John Macleod, *Scottish Theology* (Edinburgh: Banner of Truth Trust, 2015), p. 233.

[18] Patterson, *Missionary Life Among the Cannibals*, p. 56.

City Mission. While his congregation pleaded with him daily to stay, Paton began to question the legitimacy of his calling: 'Am I carrying out God's plan or my own ambition?' Yet, with friction in the air and lions in the path, Paton would not turn aside. Constrained by Christ's love and buoyed by a pious lineage, John Paton gave himself to the New Hebrides.

2

The Painful Years

I have thought of the dignity of labouring for Christ
among the heathen. To be occupied in this work is the
highest glory of men.[1]

—John Geddie, from his farewell address

I N April 1858, one month before his thirty-fourth birthday,
John Paton and his new teenage bride sailed away from
their beloved Scotland. Behind them was a homeland of
lochs and glens, before them an island of spears and blood.
They left from Greenock aboard the *Clutha* and anchored
in Melbourne before finally reaching the Aneityum Mission
on August 30. Their four-month voyage had brought them
to the New Hebrides, a group of around eighty islands in
the South Pacific. Captain James Cook first explored the
archipelago in 1773 and named them in honour of the Hebrides just off the west coast of Scotland. The islands were
subject to cyclones, earthquakes, and tidal waves—the active

[1] Patterson, *Missionary Life Among the Cannibals*, p. 62

volcano in the centre of Tanna serving as 'the best lighthouse in the world, a pillar of cloud by day and fire by night'. Many of the islands are encircled by a barrier reef a mile offshore, creating in between shallow waters of exotic blue and turquoise. With palms bending in the wind, wooded mountains peaking sharply to the sky, coconut trees lining the white beaches, and a climate of perpetual summer, the land resembled a tropical paradise. Only years of residency would unmask the island's dark side.

Captain Cook had succumbed to the dangers of the South Sea islanders. Years after discovering the New Hebrides, natives on a beach in Hawaii ran him through with spears. But his chronicles of adventure had already aroused the curiosity of the West, and by the end of the eighteenth century, the newly established London Missionary Society had decided to make the South Seas their first site of evangelistic labours.

'This is a dark land'

With Geddie and Inglis already occupying Aneityum in the south, the Patons and their co-labourers arrived on Tanna to a subdued reception. Tanna was not the South Pacific version of Malta, where, according to the Acts of the Apostles, the native people showed Paul and his companions 'unusual kindness'. Though the inhabitants of Tanna had for years used their spears to keep the outside world at bay, they welcomed the new missionaries, albeit with extreme caution. The native men were short, often less than five feet tall, with painted faces, earlobes filled with tortoise-shell rings and wooden sticks. They thought the wearing of clothes to be effeminate.[2]

Morally, the cultural practices of the New Hebrides were, as one missionary called them, 'a dead sea of pollution', such depths of Satan, Paton said, could only be found elsewhere in the first chapter of Paul's letter to the Romans. It should not be surprising that an island void of Scripture despised and degraded its women.[3] Fathers sometimes practised infanticide on their baby girls, either abandoning them in the bush or leaving them on shore at low tide. Sons of competent age were expected to strangle their widowed mothers.[4] Old women were a rarity. One chief told Paton: 'If we did not beat our women, they would never work; they would not fear and obey us; but when we have beaten, and killed, and feasted on two or three, the rest are all very quiet and good for a long time to come.'[5] Paton's son said, 'One has to live amongst the savages to realize how much the womanhood of our race owes to Jesus Christ.' He goes on to explain the lurid ways the indigenous society treated some of its young girls, sometimes incarcerating them in

[2] *Ibid.*, p. 117.

[3] For a helpful commentary on this point, see 'Women Receive Freedom and Dignity', in Alvin J. Schmidt, *How Christianity Changed the World* (Grand Rapids: Zondervan, 2004).

[4] When a chief died on the island of Efate, one of his slaves 'is slain and his body distributed, and one of his wives, usually the favourite, is buried alive with him. A deep grave is dug in which his body is laid. She takes her place at his head and commences a low wail. Part of a canoe is then inverted over her head, and the earth thrown over them.' Patterson, *Missionary Life Among the Cannibals*, p. 124.

[5] Paton, *Autobiography*, p. 97.

cages for several years. 'They are never allowed to come out, except once a day to bathe in a dish or wooden bowl placed close to each cage. They are placed in these stifling cages when quite young, and must remain there until they are young women, when they are taken out and have each a great marriage feast provided for them.'[6]

Cannibalism was practised, as were war parties and revenge killings. The victims of inter-tribal war were the rightful food of their vengeful conquerors. Patterson said, 'The natives do not hesitate to confess that, of all kinds of animal food, human flesh is the most savoury.' Theft was normal too, the shame not in stealing but in being discovered. Paton said their skill in stealing was so phenomenal that they could look you in the eye with innocence while grabbing the object with their toes and then sauntering away. 'The Tannese are born talkers', Paton would say, 'and can and will speechify on all occasions.' One well-travelled seaman described Tanna as 'the ugliest, the most indecent, the most grotesque, and the most utterly barbarous both in appearance and actual fact, of any people whom we have yet seen.'[7] In the modern day when cultural elites present God as a crutch and a needless invention, one might expect these immoral and remote islands to be free of any concept of God. The opposite was true. The islanders were like the

[6] Frank Paton, *The Kingdom in the Pacific* (London: London Missionary Society, 1913), pp. 9-10.

[7] R. Ward, ed., *Presbyterian Leaders in Nineteenth Century Australia* (Melbourne: Aust. Print Group, 1993), p. 123. As quoted in Cromarty, *King of the Cannibals*.

people of Athens, 'very religious' in every way. The islands were filled with gods as the people endlessly groped after someone greater than themselves. 'Not finding him, and not being able to live without some sort of god, they have made idols of almost everything: trees and groves, rocks and stones, springs and streams, insects and beasts, men and departed spirits, relics such as hair and finger nails, the heavenly bodies and the volcanoes.'[8]

The New Hebrides was the apex of pioneer missions. On Tanna there was no infrastructure, no written language, and no immediate access to the outside world except through the evil white traders.[9] Once a native helper from a nearby island could not fetch water because the natives had sullied the pool with the blood of a recently devoured corpse. 'This is a dark land', he said. 'The people of this land do dark works.'[10]

Man of sorrows

The Patons, the Mathiesons, Joseph Copeland and several native teachers were assigned to Tanna, an island to the

[8] Paton, *Autobiography*, p. 73.

[9] One must not belittle this latter point. The malicious activities of the European traders would bring immense pain to generations of missionaries to come. For example, when the natives of Erromanga hacked Williams and Harris to death, outrage spread through Christian Europe at such barbarity. But Frank Paton was quick to balance the scales of judgment. 'Who will blame the Erromangans? They were simply carrying out their law of revenge, and it was the best they knew. Does not the blame lie rather upon those who outraged the natives for the sake of gold? The death of Williams and Harris was the bitter fruit of the white man's sin.' F. Paton, *Kingdom in the Pacific*, p. 46.

[10] Paton, *Autobiography*, p. 68.

northeast of Aneityum where Geddie (and then Inglis) had been ministering for the past decade. Paton's task was to begin a new station on the east of Tanna at Port Resolution, where Samoans of the LMS and Aneityumese had worked off and on since 1839 with severe difficulty. John and Mary Mathieson, who had already arrived from Canada, would work the southern side of Tanna, with Copeland transitioning between the two. Paton left his wife on Aneityum with the other wives while he, Inglis, and Copeland set off for Tanna. The men arrived while the island was in the midst of another war. The discharge of muskets greeted them as armed men rushed here and there, faces painted red, black, white, and blue, with feathers protruding from their twisted hair.

That evening news came that a half a dozen men had been killed less than a mile from where they were building Paton's new home, the bodies cooked and eaten that very evening—including the wife of one of the deceased, who was strangled so that she could join her husband in the afterlife. One wonders if at this time Paton began considering Jonah's choice of Tarshish, or at least the impoverished tenements of Glasgow, and less the savage island of Tanna. It seemed as though the natives were constantly at war.

The Patons built their home on what seemed the ideal location—near the sea and upon the foundations of the old LMS cottage of Nesbit and Turner (1842).[11] Only later did they learn such close proximity to shore and inaccessibility

---

[11] *Australian Dictionary of Biography* (MUP, 1974), V:296.

to healthy trade winds made them twice as susceptible to malaria. A chief warned Paton: 'If you stay here, you will soon die! No Tanna-man sleeps so low down as you do, in this damp weather, or he too would die.' When they finally realized their error, it was too late. John unknowingly brought over his wife from Aneityum right at the start of the rainy season, where downpours would sometimes continue for weeks at a time. On February 12, 1859, Mary gave birth. Their 'island-exile thrilled with joy' over the birth of their baby boy. 'But the greatest of sorrows', John wrote, 'was treading hard upon the heels of that joy.'

Though Paton and his wife landed on Tanna on November 5, 1858, in excellent health, pneumonia and malaria struck almost immediately. On May 3, Mary Ann Paton died, aged nineteen. Their baby boy followed less than three weeks later. Paton buried them side-by-side in the same grave. Stunned, he wrote:

> Let those who have ever passed through any similar darkness as of midnight feel for me; as for all others, it would be more than vain to try to paint my sorrows. … That spot became my sacred and much-frequented shrine, during all the following months and years when I laboured on for the salvation of these savage islanders amidst difficulties, dangers, and death. But for Jesus, and the fellowship he vouchsafed me there, I must have gone mad and died beside that lonely grave.[12]

[12] *Ibid.*, p. 80. 'Whenever Tanna turns to the Lord, and is won for Christ, men in after days will find the memory of that spot still green where with ceaseless

Soon after her death, Bishop Selwyn and Rev. J. C. Patteson (who was afterwards martyred in Melanesia) visited Paton on Tanna, weeping and praying with him beside his wife's grave. They encouraged him to leave the island for a while to rest and recover. But despite such unimaginable grief, Paton resolved to stay at this post of duty. 'The courage to risk the loss was one thing', John Piper observes. 'But the courage to experience loss and press on alone was supernatural.'[13] The tenacity he learned in his father's home and the pluck he nurtured in the slums of Glasgow would now bolster him when lesser men would have packed up and quit. 'Feeling immovably assured that my God and Father was too wise and loving to err in anything that he does or permits, I looked up to the Lord for help, and struggled on in his work.'[14]

He persevered, though the trials were only beginning. He not only endured malaria more than a dozen times, but withstood it in the knowledge that this was the very disease that took the lives of his wife and child. The natives cooled to him as the novelty of his arrival wore off. The other missionaries urged him to leave if not but for a short rest. Paton refused. On he went, fearing even the briefest of respites would hinder his return.

His most faithful Christian friend was Abraham, a native from Aneityum who was loyal to him until the end. Once,

---

prayers and tears I claimed that land for God in which I had "buried my dead" with faith and hope.'

[13] John Piper, *John G. Paton: You Will Be Eaten By Cannibals!* (Minneapolis: Desiring God Foundation, 2012), p. 8.

[14] Paton, *Autobiography*, p. 85.

while building a new home on higher ground, Paton felt his life ebbing away as he climbed the knoll.

> When about two-thirds up the hill, I became so faint that I concluded I was dying. Lying down on the ground, sloped against the root of a tree to keep me from rolling to the bottom, I took farewell of old Abraham, of my mission work, and of everything around! In this weak state I lay, watched over by my faithful companion, and fell into a quiet sleep.[15]

He recovered, but oh the courage it took to endure these trials year after year. While the current world obsesses about comfort and tranquillity, Paton embodies the Pauline spirit: 'We are afflicted in every way, but not crushed; perplexed, but not driven to despair … struck down, but not destroyed' (2 Cor. 4:8-9).

He set about to learn the language, teach the people the Scriptures, and bind up their wounds after incessant battles. In time, he helped establish six missionary stations, manned by converted cannibals from neighbouring Aneityum.

He also made progress in Tannese Scripture translations. Part of his task was to teach the basics. He offered a red shirt to the first person that could memorize the alphabet. The chief won. The headman proudly squatted down and showed others how he had put the assignment to memory: "'A' is a man's legs with the body cut off … "E" is a man with one club under his feet and another over his head; "F" is a man

---

[15] *Ibid.*, p. 106.

with a large club and a smaller one.' Even the alphabet was a dangerous affair!

The violent opposition never let up, not only against Paton and his colleagues but against the native teachers as well. There were many saints and evangelists from nearby islands who were martyred by their own people for the cause of Christ. Few this side of heaven recall their names, but they stand in heaven alongside the great cloud of witnesses.

In the midst of danger, some on Tanna emerged as friends. Kowia was a faithful companion and a former cannibal who died while on Tanna. Nowar later became a dear confidant, though early on he was vacillating, always wavering, his faith weak but visible.

The men threatened Paton's life not only with the killing-stone or musket, but also with sorcery. *Nahak* was the island's black magic the sacred men would use to kill their enemies by chanting incantations over a scrap of food their victim had discarded. In an effort to debunk this folly, Paton bit into three pieces of fruit, handed them to the sorcerers and dared them to kill him with nahak. Like Elijah on Mount Carmel he ridiculed their failed attempts: 'Be quick! Stir up your gods to help you! I am not killed yet; I am perfectly well!' A week later, with victory in hand, Paton declared:

> Yes, truly; my Jehovah God is stronger than your gods. He protected me, and helped me; for he is the only living and true God, the only God that can hear or answer prayer from the children of men. Your gods cannot hear prayers,

but my God can and will hear and answer you, if you will give heart and life to him, and love and serve him only. This is my God, and he is also your friend if you will hear and follow his voice.[16]

'Alone, yet not alone!'

A general move toward Christianity in 1860–61 was halted by a measles epidemic that wiped out large portions of the population, a disease that some surmise was intentionally imported by traders. The native teachers who survived fled to Aneityum. Only Abraham remained with Paton, pledging to live and die with him in the work of the Lord. Soon, however, a new missionary couple arrived, Samuel Fulton Johnston and his wife Elizabeth, and Paton's spirits revived. This rejuvenation was short-lived. On New Year's Day, 1861, a group of intruders violently attacked Paton and Johnston as they parted ways after an evening meal. After his dogs fought off the invaders, Paton, being accustomed to such things, slept soundly that night. The Johnstons, however, were unhinged. After two weeks of insomnia, Johnston slipped into a coma, his teeth fixed in tetanus. On January 21, three weeks after the attack, Johnston died. It is unclear whether his death stemmed from the trauma of the event, an overdose of laudanum, cerebral malaria, or another factor. Nonetheless, Paton made his friend's coffin, dug the grave, and laid him to rest beside his own dear wife and child. Elizabeth Johnston left

[16] *Ibid.*, p. 142.

for Aneityum but—as a testament to supernatural determination—her journey as a missionary would continue. After three years of teaching on Aneityum, she married Joseph Copeland, Paton's Glasgow ministry partner who had escorted him to the New Hebrides.[17]

Paton reflected upon the inscrutable plans of God:

> The labourers are few and the harvest is great, and Mr Johnston was full of youth, life and activity; and why he should be safely brought over a long voyage, enabled to acquire the language, so as to be able to speak to the people, and called away when his usefulness was just beginning, must remain among the inscrutable mysteries of God.[18]

As the missionary cemetery grew, the labourers dwindled; four months later, more deaths followed. This time it was the martyrdom of George and Ellen Gordon, Canadian missionaries on the neighbouring island of Erromanga. Gordon wrote to Paton in February about the danger on the island yet assumed the worst was past. But on May 20, the islanders ambushed the couple, nearly severing Mrs Gordon's head with a tomahawk. When news of the massacre reached Paton's island of Tanna, a riot of jubilation ensued, the islanders shouting: 'Our love to the Erromangans! Our love to the Erromangans!' Though the Gordons' death seemed in vain at the time, the ichor flowing from these wounds would

---

[17] Peter Barnes observes that because the early Presbyterian missionaries possessed practical and unromantic views of marriage, 'it is not surprising to find that… [she] married the only bachelor in the missionary group'. Peter Barnes, *Aneityum*, p. 56.

[18] Patterson, *Missionary Life Among the Cannibals*, p. 441.

only serve to bring more and more missionaries, including Gordon's very own brother.[19] One converted islander later recounted:

> We fled to the caves and to the mountains, and the land of Erromanga was indeed dark. But the ship came again, and a missionary came ashore. It was Misi Gordon's brother, and oh, how our hearts leapt for joy to see him. He built his home in another place, and he became our father and our teacher, but alas! one day as he sat in his study revising the Book of Acts, which his brother had turned into our language, two natives came behind and struck him that he died. Our hearts were very, very sore, and once more the darkness was very great in the land of Erromanga. But still the ship came again [with more missionaries]. The danger was very great, but they were willing to die for us.[20]

As the threats on Paton's life continued, one wonders how his mind kept from snapping. 'He never knew when his house would be surrounded with angry natives or his party would be ambushed along the way. How do you survive when there is no kickback time? No unwinding. No sure

[19] J. D. Gordon published a memoir of his brother under the regrettable title *The Last Martyr of Erromanga*. He was later martyred on the same island on May 1, 1872. At the time of the attack, Gordon had just finished revising Acts 7 and the martyrdom of Stephen. Margaret Paton wrote that the ink was still wet on the page when James was called outside to join the noble company of those martyred in the Lord's service. But all was not in vain. Later, Paton would write: 'Erromanga is now a Christian island. There are 300 communicants, 12 elders, 40 native teachers, and 1,750 attending the schools—practically the whole population.' Paton, *Autobiography*, p. 494.

[20] F. Paton, *Kingdom in the Pacific*, p. 47.

refuge on earth.'[21] He slept with his clothes on, ready to run at a moment's notice. At times, the only thing stopping the natives was his little dog Clutha. 'God made them fear this precious creature, and often used her in saving our lives.'[22]

In January 1862, a civil war on Tanna began, bringing the danger to its zenith. Previously Paton had refused to leave because he feared all of his labour in evangelism and translation would be lost. But now he began to realize he could stay no longer. The people of Tanna refused to leave their nefarious ways. 'Our fathers loved and followed it', said one chief. 'We love and follow it, and if the Worship condemns it, we will kill you and destroy the Worship.' Those that 'hated the Worship' feared only a British man-of-war coming to their island and blowing it to bits. When this didn't happen, the natives were emboldened to turn up the heat on the missionaries.

Now on the run, Paton left all his belongings and escaped overland where a friendly chief hid him up a large tree. As the Puritans have said, when God lays men on their backs, they look up to heaven. With danger below, Paton looked upward:

> The hours I spent there live all before me as if it were but of yesterday. I heard the frequent discharging of muskets, and the yells of the savages. Yet I sat there among the branches, as safe in the arms of Jesus. Never, in all my sorrows, did my Lord draw nearer to me, and speak more soothingly in

[21] Piper, *John G. Paton*, p. 10.
[22] Paton, *Autobiography*, p. 178.

my soul, than when the moonlight flickered among these chestnut leaves, and the night air played on my throbbing brow, as I told all my heart to Jesus. Alone, yet not alone! If it be to glorify my God, I will not grudge to spend many nights alone in such a tree, to feel again my Saviour's spiritual presence, to enjoy his consoling fellowship. If thus thrown back upon your own soul, alone, all, all alone, in the midnight, in the bush, in the very embrace of death itself, have you a Friend that will not fail you then?[23]

After four years on the island, Paton saw what society would look like without any gospel trace.

To have actually lived amongst the heathen and seen their life gives a man a new appreciation of the power and blessings of the gospel, even where its influence is only very imperfectly allowed to guide and restrain the passions of men. Oh, what will it be when all men in all nations love and serve the glorious Redeemer![24]

At this time Paton experienced the grief of a Judas-like betrayal. Sirawia once had been warm to the missionaries, but now he was leading a party of cannibals to take his friend's life. Paton said, 'Sirawia, I love you all. You must know that I sought only your good. I gave you medicine and food when you and your people were sick and dying under measles; I gave you the very clothing you wear. Am I not your friend? Have we not often drunk tea and eaten together in my house?

[23] *Ibid.*, p. 200.
[24] *Ibid.*, p. 219.

Can you stand there and see your friend shot?'[25] Again, the Lord protected Paton.

His last awful night on Tanna was also the scene of God's miraculous, sovereign care. While Paton and the Mathiesons slept, Clutha sprang up in warning that murderous natives had surrounded the mission house. The missionaries crouched among the shadows in hushed prayer as the Tannese set fire to the adjacent church building and the reed fence connecting it to their dwelling.

Knowing they would soon be engulfed in the flames, Paton convinced Mathieson to open the door quickly and then lock it behind him. As he rushed out to cut down the burning fence, he was soon surround by the bloodthirsty mob. 'Kill him', they thundered!

At that dread moment came a rushing and roaring from the South, escorted with crashes of thunder and lightning. All knew this was one of the island's awful cyclones. But God is not sparing in aid toward his children. Not only did the wind extinguish the flames. It blew them *away* from the house, only to be followed by torrents of rain, making it impossible to reignite the buildings. God's hand was still on the helm.

The significance of the events never escaped Paton. He knew that the same God who had delivered Sisera into the hands of Israel was fighting for him. As the panicked natives slinked back into the bush, they cried, 'This is Jehovah's rain. Truly their God is fighting for them.' As the rain continued

[25] *Ibid.*, p. 205.

to pour, Paton and his missionary partners were left alone with arms upstretched to Jesus, basking in the joy of his faithful watch over them.

The Mathiesons, the only other missionaries now on the island, were cracking beneath the pressure. Though they managed to escape the island, Mary Mathieson died of tuberculosis a few weeks later on March 11, 1862, in the home of her uncle John Geddie. Under the weight of unbearable grief, her husband followed some months later.[26] The fragrant memory of these faithful souls would remain with Paton all his life.

By the time he boarded the sandalwood vessel *Blue Bell* sailing for Aneityum in the spring of 1862, Paton was thirty-eight years old. That same year, Hudson Taylor had broken the long-established missionary tradition in China by abandoning European dress and lifestyle. Paton could relate with Taylor's decision, for he too was forced to renounce everything, save a few portions of Scripture translations. Dead were his wife and child, the Gordons, the Mathiesons, their little daughter Minnie, Fulton Johnston, and dozens of native teachers. 'After their death', he would later write, 'I was the only one left alive in all the New Hebrides Mission north of Aneituym to tell the story of those pioneer years, during which were sown the seeds of what is now fast becoming a glorious harvest.'

---

[26] Incidentally, Mathieson's tragic death came exactly fifty years after another missions calamity—though of a different kind. Twelve years of missionary toil were destroyed when on March 11, 1812, a print shop containing William Carey's Indian dictionaries and Scripture translations went up in flames.

Who can know for sure what painful thoughts pierced his mind as he sailed away from Tanna. 'Will I ever return? Have I failed? Was I at fault? Who will go?' His labour was not totally in vain. There were, as he liked to say, streaks of dawn amidst the deeds of darkness. But from the human standpoint his four years on Tanna brought little success. It would be years before the seeds planted on that lonely island would sprout. The candle was snuffed out but the candlestick remained.

World travels

Paton had a gift for galvanizing interest in world missions. He spent the next four years doing mobilization work in Australia and Europe, raising funds for new missionaries, native workers, and a mission ship for the New Hebrides. He pled the cause of the mission, his constant prayer that at least a single missionary would one day occupy every island in the group.

Even after the horrors of the previous four years, he records almost nothing of rest. After a 1,400-mile voyage in awful conditions, he finally reached Sydney. He knew no one there. With nowhere to go and no contacts with whom to plead his cause, Paton was struck with unprecedented discouragement, wishing he had died with his dear wife on the islands. Surely, he thought, there were others more suited for such a task. But he persevered. How ironic to see this great missionary, whose *Autobiography* would make him a household name and a dinner guest with such men as George Müller and C. H. Spurgeon, securing his first audience by following a group of children into an unknown church and begging the pastor for ten minutes to address them. From there the floodgates of interest were opened and thus began Paton's remarkable and most successful four-year missionary tour of Australia and beyond.

He visited nearly every Presbyterian congregation in southern Australia, speaking 265 times in 250 days in Victoria alone, using the drama of his three and a half years on Tanna as the basis for his pleas. All of the meetings he arranged himself. His ability to inspire and compel was now on display and would become even clearer later in life as he became a kind of missionary statesman. He criss-crossed the cities and marched through the primitive outback, addressing people by the hundreds and the thousands, sometimes preaching in the open air. Many of the Australian roads in those days were crude pathways, and it was easy to walk forty miles without seeing man or home. Paton pressed on, by train, buggy, or on foot; his bag of curios slung over his shoulder.

In his *Autobiography* he rarely if ever mentions the Scripture texts used in his addresses, though the *Brisbane Courier* in 1886 reported that he preached from Acts 16:9 and the Macedonian Call. Instead, he focused on the needs of the New Hebrides, interspersed with God's biblical commands to obey. This may have stemmed from the influence of his brother James, who encouraged his brother not to preach normal sermons while travelling the globe. 'John, you should just begin straight away and tell what you have seen and experienced in your

JOHN G. PATON

work in the islands, and what the natives say and do—that is what the people want to hear. They can get sermons every Sunday, but not living statements of the doings of the Lord in the islands of the sea.'[27]

He targeted the children by encouraging them to buy shares in the mission ship for Jesus, and in time he raised sufficient funds for the beautiful new mission ship, *Dayspring*. He was as controversial as he was stubborn. An ardent sabbatarian, he refused to use public transportation on Sundays, often walking long distances between his church meetings. 'No tramcar conductor, no railway porter, no busman will ever stand up in the Judgment and say, "You robbed me of my Sabbath."'

Ironically, it was not Bible translation or the evangelization of the islands that Paton called his chief work. Instead it was awaking interest among Christians for the perishing cannibals of the New Hebrides.

> Often times, while passing through the perils and defeats of my first four years in the mission field of Tanna, I wondered … why God permitted such things. But on looking back now, I already clearly perceive … that the Lord was thereby preparing me for … the best work of all my life, namely, the kindling of the heart of Australian Presbyterianism with a living affection for these islanders of their own Southern Seas.[28]

[27] A. K. Langridge and Frank Paton, *John G. Paton: Later Years and Farewell* (London: Hodder and Stoughton, 1910) p. 247.

[28] Paton, *Autobiography*, pp. 222-23.

Hudson Taylor of China said that God's work, done in God's way, will never lack God's supply. Paton concurred. Among his goals in travelling was to show that 'the finger of God is as visible still, to those who have eyes to see, as when the fire-cloud pillar led his people through the wilderness'. This is similar to Paton's contemporary George Müller, who admitted his chief reason for starting the orphan work was so the natural eye could *see* that God could really be trusted to meet the needs of his children.[29]

Once, when journeying by carriage, a fellow Scotsman asked if Paton was a minister. When he said yes, the catechizing began:

'Where is your church?'
'I have no church …'
'Where is your home?'
'I have no home.'
'Where have you come from ?'
'The South Sea Islands.'
'What are you doing in Australia?'
'Pleading the cause of the mission.'
'Are you a Presbyterian?'
'I am'.[30]

When his task was finished in Australia, he took a three-month voyage to Britain to stir up additional missionary

[29] See John Piper, 'George Müller's Strategy for Showing God' (2004 Bethlehem Conference for Pastors; Minneapolis: Desiring God, 2004).
[30] Paton, *Autobiography*, p. 243.

interest. En route his ship entered a thunderstorm and was struck by lightning. Paton was so injured he had to be carried to his cabin. Later, while travelling by steamer in the dead of a Scottish winter, we get a glimpse of Paton's sharp hostility to alcohol. When a storm arose, everyone was ordered down below. The atmosphere was so full of whisky and tobacco that Paton begged the captain for permission to sit on deck. 'You'll be washed overboard', he warned, but upon hearing the missionary's pleas, his sailors literally tied Paton to the mast. Such exposure to the cold caused his foot to go numb. When feeling would not return to his foot for weeks, the doctors prescribed amputation. God heard Paton's prayers, however, and his foot eventually recovered.

His reunion with his parents was heavenly and yet full of tears, as they reminisced over that grave on Tanna which 'held mother and son locked in each other's embrace till the Resurrection Day'. His reunion with his in-laws was agonizing. While they greeted him warmly without any murmuring toward their Lord, the heartbreak over the loss of their dear daughter and grandson was severe. Paton confided they never recovered.

Meanwhile, the Reformed Presbyterian Church in Scotland honoured Paton's faithful work on the islands by granting him the distinguished appointment as Moderator of their highest court.

Paton married Margaret Whitecross on June 17, 1864. She came from a godly family, her brother a missionary, her sister a pastor's wife, and her father a Christian author. He and his new bride made a final visit to his pious parents before departing again for the South Seas. The couple knelt before the venerable patriarch, snow-white locks streaming down his shoulders, as he interceded for his son. 'It was the last time that ever on this earth those accents of intercession, loaded with a pathos of deathless love, would fall upon my ears. I knew to a certainty that when we rose from our knees and said farewell, our eyes would never meet again till they were flooded with the lights of the Resurrection Day.'[31] His parents, as they had before, gave away their son again with a free heart, though not without the sword of loss and anguish piercing their hearts. Paton's mother, always more restrained than her husband, composed herself until her son was out of sight, only then to heave cries that only a mother can know.

[31] *Ibid.*, p. 286.

Margaret Whitecross Paton.

3

The Fruitful Years

> My soul soared upward after his, and all the harps of God
> seemed to thrill with song as Jesus presented to the Father
> this trophy of redeeming love ... mingling our tears with
> Christian natives ... who only a few years before was a
> blood-stained cannibal, and whom now we mourned as
> a brother, a saint, an apostle amongst his people.[1]
>
> —John G. Paton

A FTER a 'fast trip' of three months from London to Australia, the Patons landed in Sydney on December 27, 1864, having sighted land just twice. Maggie's mother apparently escorted them on the trip, though perhaps not surprisingly, Paton never mentions this in his *Autobiography*.

Upon arrival, he immediately faced two challenges. The first was the matter of funds for the *Dayspring*, a beautiful two-masted sailing ship recently purchased by the faithful prayers and children's pennies from around the world. While

---

[1] On the death of Namakei, his first Aniwan convert. Paton, *Autobiography*, p. 393.

the amount he raised was beyond the goal, it was insufficient for the necessary upkeep of £1,000 *per anum*. He thus pressed the church of Australia to do their part, not just Nova Scotia and Scotland. Soon the money poured in, the yearly upkeep once again provided chiefly by the children's Sunday School. Truly remarkable is the fact that Paton raised over £7,000 in his worldwide travels, which was nearly sixty times his income of £120 *per annum*.

Curaçoa Incident

The second difficulty entailed the bad press regarding the bombardment of Port Resolution, Tanna, by *H.M.S. Curaçoa* in 1865. As it happened, some of the New Hebrides missionaries had summoned the proper authorities to address the ill treatment of the missionaries on the islands, including the murder of the Gordons on Erromanga. A British man-of-war—with Paton and Inglis on board as translators and the *Dayspring* in tow—visited many of the islands, summoning the chiefs on board and urging them to behave. On Tanna, however, the chiefs refused to talk. After fair warning, canons shelled uninhabited portions of Port Resolution. But when it was all over, a handful of natives had died.

Public outrage was immediate. An illustration in an Australian newspaper implied the missionaries were supportive—the eye-catching headline 'Gospel and Gunpowder' plastered across the page. Paton was forced on the defensive from the beginning, calling himself 'the best abused man in all Australia'.

The opinions of the New Hebrides missionaries were divided over the morality of the action. John Geddie, who was in Canada during the infraction, was in strict opposition. He considered it to be in direct contradiction to the example of Christ and 'one of the most humiliating events in the history of modern missions'.[2] He charged the white men with killing far more natives than had been killed throughout their history on the islands and accused Paton of taking too dour a view of past events on Tanna. He even resigned his connection to the Presbyterian Church in Victoria when he learned they were supporting Paton.

The majority of the missionaries, however, stood with Paton's perspective, including Geddie's teammate John Inglis. Though Paton never urged the captain to shell the island and sided toward mercy, he believed Christians have the right to appeal to Caesar, as any Christian resident would if, for example, his home were to be robbed. After Paton threatened legal prosecution unless a clear apology was published, the missionaries were fully exonerated.

But the battle wasn't over. When Paton agreed to stand before the Presbytery in Sydney, Geddie claimed he would rather have his hand burned off with fire than be involved with such an event. The court applauded and urged Paton to promise he would never take part in such an event again. Instead, Paton doubled down, reclaiming his right for civil

---

[2] Patterson, *Missionary Life Among the Cannibals*, p. 474.

action.[3] 'I will never make such a promise', he said. 'I have done as clear a Christian duty as I ever did in my life. I am not ashamed. I offer no apology.'[4]

It isn't clear who was correct in the *Curaçoa* matter. Paton claimed no churches were lost who supported the Mission except those of Nova Scotia. Sadly, the work on the New Hebrides remained a stench in the nostrils of some ministers and lifelong friends back home. A few would never speak to Paton again.

Settling down

Paton, now officially appointed as a missionary from the Presbyterian churches of Australia, returned to the New Hebrides in the fall of 1866 with his wife and child. Robert, born a year earlier in Australia, was baptized on the island by John Inglis, the 'eldest and most honoured missionary'. Paton still desired to return to Tanna, but the united counsel was that he go elsewhere. One might expect a man who had won and lost so much upon those shores to find them strangely difficult to abandon. Decades later his heart still bled afresh when recounting those events. They had sailed past Tanna just long enough for the new Mrs Paton to catch a glimpse through the looking glass of two small gravestones—that sacred spot still etched upon her husband's mind. 'Oh, how

---

[3] Paton even points out Geddie's inconsistencies, for he had called for investigations upon the islands as well. Elsewhere, when a church on Aneityum was burned down, he used civil authorities to inflict thirty lashes upon the presumed perpetrator.

[4] Paton, *Autobiography*, p. 303.

I longed to spend a quiet hour by the grave of her, in whose footsteps I feel so unfit to follow, and who met her trials so unshrinkingly and alone.'[5]

They also stopped at Fotuna, briefly considering settling on that island of 700 residents. In the end they chose the hostile but less irritable island of Aniwa. It was much smaller than Tanna—barely nine miles by three—but just as beautiful with her garish brown crags contrasting with the dashing spray beneath.

For the next fifteen years, Aniwa would be the centre of Paton's missionary enterprise. Here he would enjoy the most fruitful years of his life. He referred to the island as the land wherein his past years of labour, patience, and trust were to see their fruits ripening at length.

The natives on Aniwa, though still menacing, were less dangerous than the 'slow relenting' Tannese and received the new missionaries with kindness. Paton did all he could to make life comfortable for his new bride, perhaps the first white woman to have landed on the island. She had several helpers (including a cook), some of whom even spoke broken English. Their first temporary home was a large native hut framed by reeds and sugarcane leaves. This was followed by a permanent abode, complete with French windows made from discarded mission boxes. Though it sat far from the malaria breeding grounds, it was centred

[5] Margaret Paton, *Letters from the South Seas* (Edinburgh: Banner of Truth Trust, 2003), p. 20.

in the exact place where the cannibals had feasted for ages past. One can glimpse the fortitude of the new bride as her husband filled two baskets with human bones while clearing the land.

The church of God on Aniwa

J. Graham Miller suggests something changed in Paton when he arrived on this new island, his severe preaching of the past now blunted by a tone of firmness linked with kindness: 'on Aniwa he was a new man, preaching Christ and his saving death and resurrection and seeing early response'.[6] Ministry accelerated almost immediately. If Tanna equalled the mob's disdain for Stephen in Acts, Aniwa matched the crowd's acceptance of Peter. Several of the Aniwans could understand Tannese, a great aid to Paton while they learnt the local language. 'There is no dictionary, no grammar, to refer to,' Margaret Paton confessed; 'nothing but our own ears to instruct us.' Great enthusiasm filled the home when she finally discovered the meaning of the little prefix '*ka*'. She ran to tell John. Such are the small victories that bring missionaries joy.

Twenty to thirty attended the first church service, many of them wearing the clothing that had been distributed earlier. A year later, attendance averaged 120 on Sunday morning and 60 on Wednesday. They were very careful not to baptize

---

[6] J. Graham Miller, 'Paton, John Gibson (1824–1907)' in *Australian Dictionary of Evangelical Biography*.

believers too soon, often giving the youth another year after
their salvation testimonies to show fruit so as not to shame
the name of Christ. Converts could not be baptized until they
attended a communicants' class for twelve months. At other
times they would permit baptism but disallow participation
at the Lord's Table for up to a year. New converts at once
became missionaries, their 'changed life, shining out amid
the surrounding darkness … a gospel in largest capitals' for
all to read. And what was one of the first marks of repentance the island showed? A simple form of family worship in
every house similar to what had been practised by Paton's
father in his own humble home long ago in Scotland. Paton
would later write:

> God never guided me back to Tanna, but others, my dear
> friends, have seen his kingdom planted and beginning to
> grow amongst the slowly relenting race. Aniwa was to be
> the land wherein my past years of toil and patience and faith
> were to see their fruits ripening at length. I claimed Aniwa
> for Jesus, and by the grace of God Aniwa now worships at
> the Saviour's feet.[7]

His focus remained gospel ministry. Evangelism turned
into established churches; Bible studies turned into translated
Scriptures. The whole week was a hive of ministry. After three
years, they baptized their first converts.

> At the moment when I put the bread and wine into those
> dark hands, once stained with the blood of cannibalism,

[7] Paton, *Autobiography*, p. 312.

but now stretched out to receive and partake the emblems and seals of the Redeemer's love, I had a foretaste of the joy of glory that well nigh broke my heart to pieces. I shall never taste a deeper bliss, till I gaze on the glorified face of Jesus himself.[8]

John and Margaret Paton laboured to help the islands socially as well. Margaret had spunk and humour, teaching the ladies how to sew and read. She taught them music and how to sing parts. They built two orphanages and these orphans later on would be instrumental in saving the Patons' lives from cruel plots. They also erected schools and dispensed medicine. The mission bell rang after dinner each evening to signal those needing medical assistance could come. The most destitute were also given food.

The Dayspring

In the modern era that enjoys such ease of transportation and communication, it is easy to downplay the importance of Paton's task of raising funds for a mission ship. Such a vessel, however, was crucial, not only in preventing the needless loss of devoted lives, but for the safe and efficient transport of reinforcements to the islands. The New Hebrides were so distant and obscure that without a mission vessel, missionaries would be forced to catch a ride with any barge or even slave-trading ship they could find. Here follows a brief summary of the history and benefits of the *Dayspring*.

[8] *Ibid.*, p. 376.

The Dayspring.

Though no mission ship existed when Paton and his wife arrived on the islands in 1858, he spent the four years in Australia and the United Kingdom raising funds for a missionary vessel. *Dayspring 1* was built in Nova Scotia and weighed just 120 tons, double the amount some of the more thrifty missionaries thought it should be. This little virgin schooner arrived in the New Hebrides in 1864 with John and Margaret Paton as her first passengers. Travelling aboard her was not always pleasant, but it was considerably better than on previous vessels.

Margaret spoke glowingly about the ship and put its value to the missionaries into perspective, calling it the 'one visible link between us and the Christian world'. For one to have seen the vessel's arrival as a bright day in a lonely existence, 'lying almost becalmed in the distance, with her sails spread, and a gorgeous sunset behind her, you would need to have gone through our experience in this lonely island'.

The missionaries devoured the contents of the letters, sometimes taking weeks to read them. One from Margaret's mother ran to forty-six pages! The *Dayspring* did not bring joy to all the missionaries, however. Some waited in vain, looking upon her as an instrument of cruelty. Margaret attests:

> I know of at least two mothers in this mission, who have gone to the shores of their lonely islands day after day with aching hearts, and eyes strained to catch the least little speck of hope on the horizon—for their babies were lying so sick that they feared they might die, ere the *Dayspring* came to carry them away to see the doctor.[9]

The *Dayspring* (from Luke 1:78) had become part and parcel of the islands. None of the residents could imagine life on the New Hebrides without her. So when she was wrecked off the shores of Aneityum in 1872, it was a painful blow. 'The natives all cried about it like children for weeks on end.'

Even before the devastating cyclone that wrecked her, funds were already drying up due to the high cost of maintaining such a vessel. If this were not bad enough, the mangled ship was unknowingly bought and reconstructed by a notorious Australian slave-trading company. The consequences of this loss were severe, for not only had the missionaries lost their chief means of transport, but a ship the islanders had learned to trust would now be used to lure unsuspecting natives on

[9] Margaret Paton, *Letters from the South Seas*, pp. 78-79.

board and into the slaver's net. The missionaries turned to earnest prayer. God in his grace heard their pleas and sent a gale upon the anchored ship so severe that it incapacitated her permanently. 'Daughter of the waves', Paton wrote, 'better for thee, as for thy human sisters, to die and pass away than to suffer pollution and live on in disgrace!'

Another slightly larger vessel was quickly procured, *Dayspring 2*, and ploughed the seas for the next ten years. In 1884 Paton was commissioned to raise funds for a steamship. *Dayspring 3* was launched in 1895 but was wrecked soon thereafter in 1896.

Family life

Perhaps Margaret Paton's greatest contribution to missions was her compilation of letters sent home (from 1865–89), later published under the title *Letters and Sketches.*[10] Most of what is known about the Paton home is found in this fascinating volume. It would be wise here to enumerate several ways in which her correspondence helps the reader understand life and ministry on the islands.

First, Margaret's letters help the reader understand what we might call 'the lighter side' of missionary life. Her feminine perspective on the New Hebrides balances well the rugged version of her husband's *Autobiography*. The picture she paints of domestic life is vivid, including details of vacation time, picture books, blocks of ice from Melbourne, gifts of

---

[10] Reprinted by the Trust in 2003 as Margaret Paton, *Letters from the South Seas*.

perfume, whale sightings, harmonium concerts, and views of brilliant sunsets from their veranda. She often uses the word 'romantic' to describe scenery or budding relationships, and talks of how she and John would 'stroll home arm-in-arm in the quiet of the moonlight'. She wasn't afraid to break the 'I'll stay here till I die' mould by confessing: 'I do sometimes think how nice it would be to be in civilization with a small house of our own.' In one moment she spoke of watching for hours the grand breakers crash on the shore; in another she recalls falling over in fits of mischievous laughter when her colleague fell into the river. The pervasive characteristic of the Paton home seems to have been laughter—often in recurring and irrepressible bursts. 'John and I could hardly drink our tea for laughing.'

Second, Margaret honestly addressed the painful side of home life. Tears of laughter filled their home. So also did tears of sorrow. She bore ten children on the island, four of whom died in infancy. With little medical aid, if a baby fell ill, often the only solution was to sail to Australia for assistance. It would be four months before a return could be made.

Sometimes grief would arrive with news from home. A letter arrived in Aniwa the day their son Frank was born carrying the sad news that Margaret's sister had passed away. Paton kept the letter from his wife for ten weeks until she was strong enough to receive it.

The deepest sorrow was, however, caused by the deaths of their children. The early months of 1873 brought severe trials to the Paton family. The year began with a cyclone that mowed down houses and destroyed the *Dayspring*—at that time their only tie to the outside world. This was followed weeks later by an earthquake, of which Margaret said 'the hurricane was nothing to it'. When the house began swaying from side to side at midnight, John tried to jump out of bed, but Maggie clung to him like a vice and wouldn't let go. 'Our little lambs slept calmly through it all', the bewildered mother wrote.

Then came John's sudden bout of rheumatic fever and sciatica, the latter leaving him bedridden and immobile. Meanwhile their baby girl, Helena, was born. The angel-child, as they called her, entered the world healthy and bright. It was the hot season, however, and Margaret had haemorrhaged, leaving her incapacitated after the arduous delivery. 'I would have given anything', she wrote, 'for someone from back home to come and take care of us.' Later, while trying to change the baby, she fainted and John was forced to direct the natives from his sickbed as to how to pick her up. Those few moments of chaos left the baby exposed enough to get a chill and fever. Six days after Helena was born, Maggie took the baby from the arms of her native assistant only to find the cold chill of death upon the infant's face. 'What a death-knell that sounded in my heart!' The devastated parents lay stricken in bed, calling out in tears and praying for one another from across the room.

As their young children sobbed, the parents now turned to the matter of a casket. 'We might as well have asked any of the natives to make a ship as to make a coffin.' John gave instructions to his two boys, six and four, to use their toy box as their little sister's casket. Until this moment, mother had not cried. Only after the body was taken out of house did the floodgates of emotion swing open. They returned to lay the little coffin on their mother's bed as she cried and clutched the tiny box to the sound of their father's prayers. Neither of them was strong enough to attend the funeral, but the boys' singing over the grave was within earshot of their parents. 'God only can ever know how our hearts were torn by the pathos of that event, as we lay helpless, almost dying, and listened to our children's trembling voices!'

Racked with doubt about infant salvation, her husband's theological books offered no comfort on the subject. 'We used to long so for some kind Christian friend to look in upon us; for, in time of affliction, the natives are exactly the opposite of white people', the former typically shying off instead of sympathizing.

The trials continued. Paton was so ill he could not attend church for ten weeks. At mealtime, Bob, their oldest, would sit in father's chair and say the blessing. John was sinking fast and for two days couldn't speak. Sleep wouldn't come for weeks and the faintest and most distant sounds terrorized him. When he was finally able to get up and about, Margaret said the emaciated man who was leaning on his crutch with steps an inch apart, had aged twenty years. Such were the sorrows added to sorrows.

This is not to say the Patons' were bereft of any encouragement. Many missionaries nearby offered comfort. John and Jessie Inglis on Aneityum were like a father and mother to them. The Patons so respected the Watts on Tanna ('our mainstay in every trouble') that they named one of their sons after Mr Watt: Walter Watt Paton. Incidentally, the Watt family (who arrived on Tanna seven years after Paton fled) served on the island for more than forty years. Though their ministry was not flamboyant or full of heroic success, a lesson can be taken from their perseverance. Oscar Michelsen, a contemporary missionary from Norway, said of the Watts:

> [They] do not rejoice in the same amount of success as some of the other missionaries in the group ... but they have done what no one else has done in the New Hebrides; and, perhaps, a similar case is hard to find anywhere else in the world. They have held out against the heathenism of Tanna.[11]

The much-loved native converts were also a boon. Margaret confessed that the islanders comforted the best because, like children, they did not try to sermonize suffering with blundering words.

But some sorrow can never be assuaged. Frank Paton would later write: 'There is still opportunity, even in the South Seas, to preach the gospel where it has never been preached before.' But then, as if recounting the trials his family had borne, he

[11] Oscar Michelsen, *Cannibals Won for Christ: A Story of Missionary Perils and Triumph in Tongoa, New Hebrides* (London: Morgan and Scott, 1893), p. 176.

added: 'There are still wounds to be received for him who was wounded for our transgressions.'[12]

The third benefit from Margaret Paton's journal is what may be called a 'defence' of John Paton as husband and father. This is not to say people questioned Paton's leadership in the home. Observers a century ago certainly were more forgiving when it came to the rigour and ethical dilemmas of family life on the mission field. But any reader of his *Autobiography* cannot help but be confronted with two piercing questions: Why does he give so few details about his family? Was he negligent by putting his family in harm's way?

Regarding the first question, to say that Paton was loath to lift up the veil on his family's private life would be an understatement. Though Paton wrote often about the significance of family, he was reserved regarding the particulars of his wife and children. He only mentions his first wife's name once and gives almost no details of her background. Even when a few details come regarding his first wife Mary, it stems from the obituary written by John Inglis, almost as if it would have been inappropriate for Paton to relate them himself. He doesn't tell how he met his second wife and even apologizes for disclosing one small detail of their wedding. Only a few times does he mention the names of his children.

The reader would be unwise to construe this as disinterest or fatherly incompetence. Besides the fact that Scots feel

---

[12] Langridge and F. Paton, *Kingdom in the Pacific*, p. 134.

keenly that it is in bad taste to praise one's own, there are legitimate reasons for Paton's actions. First, he most likely viewed intimate family details as inappropriate for an autobiography written for the purpose of missions mobilization. Even if he erred in keeping familial information too tight to his chest, today's narcissistic culture of hyper-transparency and full disclosure could probably take from him a valuable lesson. The test of a good family man is not the volume he speaks of wife and children but the time he spends with them. The adoration his family heaped upon him proves he succeeded with regard to the latter. Second, Margaret Paton's *Letters and Sketches* were published only five years after her husband's *Autobiography*—both of which were edited by John's brother James. It is reasonable to surmise they agreed he would address the ministry and she the family.

This leads to the second question: Was Paton irresponsible in the way he exposed his family to danger? Margaret Paton never even hints at frustration in this regard. 'I do not know how it is, and can't account for such feelings, as my own mission life was decidedly happy.' Instead, she only loads on him tremendous respect—calling him 'the kindest husband in the world'. Remember that these letters were not written for publication but began as personal letters to friends and family. Such private correspondence would have presented the perfect setting in which to vent her complaints. Instead, she wrote: 'I often think John a perfect saint, indeed, in his whole-hearted consecration, and singleness of aim for God's glory in the conversion of the heathen; and yet he is delight-fully *human,* if you rub him up the wrong way.'[13]

She rebuked those who chastised missionaries for bringing a family with them to a dangerous land. 'Our bairns are little missionaries, every one', she wrote, and thanked God for her children, not only for the happiness they brought but for the help in ministry and the daily object lesson of the gospel before the heathen which they embodied.

Letters of pure gold

A story unto themselves is that of the missionary wives on the New Hebrides—saints so easily forgotten yet indispensable to the work. They were made from solid cloth. Among them was Mrs Jessie Inglis, who on one occasion asked a missionary colleague what she was reading. Her friend quickly dismissed the question, citing her hectic schedule of housework and babies. Jessie countered: 'Read no books! And what do you think you will become? Your husband is a great reader; he is reading daily; and if you read none, will you be any companion to him ten years hence? No, do what you like but you must read.'[14]

On an island where women were degraded and discarded, the missionary wives served as living monuments to the change that comes through Christ. Geddie writes: 'It is chiefly through the instrumentality of the missionary's wife,

[13] Margaret Paton, *Letters from the South Seas*, p. 263.
[14] Quoted, Murray, *Scottish Christian Heritage*, p. 232.

that those of her own sex are to be raised from the depths of degradation and misery, and elevated to the position that God has assigned them.'[15] When the Scriptures and the Spirit work in tandem within the human soul, women are raised in honour before their families, not lowered as slaves in the harems of their husbands.

Perhaps the greatest eulogy to the unspeakable heroism of the missionary wives comes from Paton's own son. Frank spoke candidly about the noble share of toil and sacrifice these women bore—far from the cultured societies and warmth of relatives. He wrote:

> The green hillsides that rise from its blue waters show here and there a gleam of white—the coral graves of the sainted women who laid down their lives for Christ's black children. The full story can never be written in the pages of human literature, but every word of it is written in letters of pure gold in the heavenly records of the Son of Man.[16]

Among the greatest trials these women bore was the breakup of the home. As the Paton children grew it was necessary for them to leave home to attend school in Australia. 'My heart's just like to break,' Margaret wrote, 'when I think of all their little ways, and I can't be with them!' It was difficult to confide with any of the native ladies about the sorrow she felt. How could they understand? But later on they *did* understand when sending off their own children to

---

[15] Patterson, *Missionary Life Among the Cannibals*, p. 357.
[16] F. Paton, *Kingdom in the Pacific*, p. 70.

other islands to be native teachers. 'Missi, you did not think we felt like you. You never told us your troubles, You used to smile, when you spoke of your children in the far-off land, when we knew your heart was crying out for them. We knew the language of your heart, Missi, though you tried to hide it from us; and we mothers often cried about you!'[17]

The bouts of suffering continued as well. Writing back home on January 1, 1881, Margaret recounts the painful days of the previous year. She suffered for five months night and day from painful rheumatism, diphtheria, and bedsores. Once she was reduced to a skeleton, her family held round-the-clock prayer vigils. Most, including her husband, thought her time had come. But when sixteen-year-old Bob rushed home from Australia, she rallied. The sight of her towering son whom she had not seen for three years revived her waning soul. Death was in the cup and very nearly swallowed, but God once again dispensed mercy to the Paton family.

The same was not true for their son Walter. In the same year, Papa's 'wee shadow' entered eternity at two years of age. So high was the anguish, Margaret said, 'I have sometimes feared it would sweep away our reason.' John was devastated, rarely eating and pacing the floor for hours at night. Later that year they left Aniwa. Their fifteen years of day-by-day ministry on the island had come to a close. It would be eight years before they would visit the island again.

[17] Margaret Paton, *Letters from the South Seas*, p. 292.

4

The Final Years

> In all my work amongst the natives, I have striven to train
> them to be self-supporting, and have never helped them
> where I could train them to help themselves.[1]
>
> —John G. Paton

PATON was now embarking on a new phase of his life, a shift away from being a primitive evangelist to a kind of worldwide missionary statesman. Preaching to those with tomahawks and war paint was out; inspiring those in gaiters and spats was in. His greatest work of promoting the Presbyterian mission around the world was about to begin.

Travels

Three separate journeys to America and the United Kingdom would occupy the majority of his time for the next seventeen years. The first journey took place in 1884 when he was commissioned to go to Great Britain and Ireland to raise £6,000 for a steamship. He toiled as vigorously in raising funds in

[1] Paton, *Autobiography*, p. 363.

Europe as he did in evangelizing the islands. Now sixty years old, Paton was still robust—not unlike the aged Caleb (cf. Josh. 14:11). By the time he returned to Australia in October 1885, he had raised £9,000. Around this time, due to his brother's pleadings, Paton began penning his *Autobiography*. The first edition appeared in 1889 and the entire print run sold out in just two days. The consecrated life of John and the masterly edits of his brother James made the book a success. In 1891, he saw the founding of the interdenominational 'John G. Paton Fund'. In the same year he was granted an honorary doctorate by the University of Edinburgh. His portrait was painted by the great Australian artist Tom Roberts, and was put on the wall of the Assembly Hall in Melbourne. John Paton was now a household name.

Paton was a profoundly emotional man. He felt deeply the love and sacrifices of those faithful supporters overseas. After spending several weeks in Glasgow, raising support and urging young men to give their lives to missions, Paton, now sixty-one and on the cusp of his departure, was standing on the platform of a packed church building. Instead of shaking hands with the large congregation, Paton walked down the centre aisle as everyone stood, each one giving their final benediction as he passed: 'God bless you.' 'We are praying.' 'Godspeed.' Paton was deeply moved and humbled. He said:

> To one who had striven and suffered less, or who less appreciated how little we can do for others compared with what Jesus had done for us, this scene might have ministered to

spiritual pride; but long ere I reached the door of that hall, my soul was already prostrated at the feet of my Lord in sorrow and in shame that I had done so little for him, and I bowed my head and could have gladly bowed my knees to cry, 'Not unto us; Lord, not unto us!'[2]

From 1886 to 1892 Paton travelled through Australia, raising funds for the mission and plying his 'one talent' (as he would say) by pleading the cause of the islands. Many missionaries labouring in other heathen lands gave themselves to the work having first heard from him the report of God's work in the New Hebrides.

His second major worldwide voyage began in 1892 and was part of a campaign to prohibit the dreaded Kanaka Traffic which was depopulating the islands. This traffic involved the systematic deception of men from the islands who were procured for and forced to labour in the sugar fields of Australia and Fiji. The traffickers were paid a price 'per head' for each muscular native they could provide the plantations. Eventually slave trading was 'banned', but in reality it was only camouflaged by regulations. The traffick continued to thrive for years hurting the mission's work because the natives became embittered against the white men who had deceitfully clapped their neighbours in irons. 'You may not care for their agony,' Paton wrote, 'but God hears the cries, sees the tears, pities the agony, and will surely avenge the murder of our downtrodden, defenceless islanders.'[3]

---

[2] Paton, *Autobiography*, p. 440.
[3] Langridge and F. Paton, *Later Years and Farewell*, p. 99.

Later, as the slave trade waned, the import of alcohol and firearms increased. Paton also opposed this vigorously. He wrote:

> It is sad indeed to see the cruel white man, first by the Kanaka Traffic and now by drink, vice, and deadly weapons, reducing a noble race from 150,000 a few years ago to some 90,000 or so now, a decrease that is due to these destroying evils. It pains me exceedingly to see our successful and glorious Christian mission work thus retarded, and the natives ruined by white traders and the curses of civilization.[4]

The islands were being exploited. Change could happen if someone went to America and persuaded the authorities there to prevent the trade in intoxicants and firearms to the islands. And who better to prick the Christian conscience than the sixty-eight-year-old John G. Paton? Gentle externally, he burned with indignation over the misuse of 'his people', as he liked to describe the natives. He wrote in July 1892: 'I go to America to get her if possible to agree to prevent her traders using intoxicants and firearms on the islands.' But the goal of his journey was more than lobbying politicians and gathering collections for the mission. This 'was never my primary aim; but always the saving of souls, by the story of the New Hebrides. For that cause I would gladly die.'

Thus began what he called his 'Tour Round the World in the Cause of Jesus'. His voyage to San Francisco set the torrid pace he would keep for the next two years. He devoted

[4] *Ibid.*, p. 18.

eight hours a day to copying translations and finishing his dictionary of the Aniwan language.

He went on to address nearly 1,400 audiences. He spoke not only before the greatest universities of America and England but also visited the world's leading Western diplomats, pleading with them to forbid the sale of firearms and intoxicants that were now streaming into the islands. He received more invitations to speak than he could answer, his newly published autobiography offering unprecedented opportunities.

The snowy-haired missionary typically held three meetings every Sunday and one per day during the week. Paton was never one to waste time. Writing from New York on April 1, 1893:

> I am not losing an hour. My audiences range from three hundred to three thousand or more and a deeper interest is being awakened in foreign missions. I hope, too, that some are being led to Jesus for salvation. I long to see you all, and then to return to my dear Aniwans for a refreshing time, and to give them a new start in the Lord's work.[5]

During his visit to Chicago he resided just steps away from the World's Fair but he did not attend. It held no attraction for him, later telling inquisitive friends back home that he was too overwhelmed with mission work even to care about it.

The constant round of train stations and strange beds never shifted his focus. 'Dear madam, you are very kind. The

[5] *Ibid.*, p. 31.

Lord bless and reward you', he would say, as some urgent and influential hostess pleaded with him to take a drive in her carriage for an airing. To another he might say, 'I beg of you to excuse me. I have the mission interests to attend to, and my letters to answer, and if you will let me away to my room quietly, I shall be so grateful.'

Donations for the mission's ship flooded in. Sometimes as many as seventy communications per day would arrive, enclosed with money with notes such as: 'From a working-man who prays for God's blessing on you and work like yours every day in family worship.' If people insisted the gift go to him personally, he flatly refused the gift. With so much money passing through this poor missionary's fingers, one wonders if ever envy crept in. Indeed, it seemed the only emotion to be awakened was one of sanctified jealousy. When one wealthy businessman kept his company running for no other reason than to support God's cause, Paton wrote: 'God, who knows me, sees that I have never coveted money for myself or my family; but I did envy that Christian merchant the joy that he had in having money, and having the heart to use it as a steward of the Lord Jesus!'[6]

The effusion of joy that accompanied so many of the financial gifts is overwhelming—the pathos and emotion is almost tangible. Common are statements such as: 'I have prayed for you every day since.' 'God has prospered me.' 'This is one

[6] Paton, *Autobiography*, p. 428.

of the happiest moments of my life, when I am now able to give you another little bit of paper.'

Meanwhile, in 1894, while Paton was away, Margaret left Sydney to visit their son Fred, now serving as a missionary on Malekula Island in the New Hebrides. He had 'not lost an iota of his fun and energy' but his home needed a woman's touch 'everywhere' as he was at the time living in 'noble loneliness'. It was obvious that her son had inherited the daring of his parents. 'Fred does not know what fear means, and sleeps with his doors and windows wide open all night.' Wondering how she would leave her missionary son alone on the island, she wrote:

> It is nothing comparatively to give one's self to the mission. It *is* something to give one's children, and I begin to have some conception of what it was for our Father in heaven to give up his own Son unto the death.[7]

John Geddie had similar sentiments. After he and his wife decided to send their eldest daughter back to Britain, he wrote: 'The most painful sacrifices which missionaries are called on to suffer in these islands is separation from their children, whose interest and welfare demand their removal to a less polluted moral atmosphere.'[8]

[7] Langridge and F. Paton, *Later Years and Farewell*, p. 90.

[8] Patterson, *Missionary Life Among the Cannibals*, p. 105. He would later explain why he sent her home. 'I am following the advice and example of other missionaries. The experiment of training up children amid the abominations of heathenism in the Pacific, has already been tried, and the result, in many cases, has been painfully disastrous. Of all trials which missionaries in these islands are called on to encounter,

In September 1894 Paton left New York and sailed for the United Kingdom. Great enthusiasm awaited him, most notably in his homeland of Scotland. On one occasion he was asked to preach at the chapel of his alma mater at the University of Glasgow. The students were in awe that the famous missionary to the cannibals had once occupied their seat of learning. The congregation was crowded to excess. During the question and answer time, a professor stood and proclaimed: 'Had I been a cannibal, one look at Dr Paton's benignant and noble face would have made me a vegetarian to the end of my days!' Acute flattery, certainly, but the humorous remark brought down the house.

By August 1894 Paton was sailing back to Australia. He had played a crucial role in abolishing the Kanaka Traffic, though this dark chapter of bloodshed would not officially end until 1901. He had also raised enough funds to build and maintain a new steamship, *Dayspring 3*, which launched on August 19, 1895. At seventy-two years of age, Paton escorted one of the ship's first passengers, Mr and Mrs Frank Paton, who had been newly assigned to the island of Tanna—where Frank's father had received his baptism of fire as a missionary. Though the island had received missionaries in the interim, it had remained largely unconquered.

On October 1, 1896, on only the fourth voyage of *Dayspring 3*, the ship ran aground upon an uncharted reef. The

---

that of separation from their dear offspring is the most painful. This is one of the stern duties to which we are called by him who says, "He that loveth son or daughter more than me is not worthy of me."' (p. 219.)

crew was saved but the hopes, gifts, sacrifice, and years of toil that were represented in that ship sank beneath the waves. The aged missionary no doubt struggled to understand the devastating news, but resigned this trial, as all others, to the all-wise purposes of God.

In 1899, Paton took his third and final 'round the world' journey at the age of seventy-six. His journey to the United States and Great Britain continued with the same 'spirit of consecrated energy', speaking often to gatherings in the thousands. He travelled over 44,000 miles on this final trip, addressing 820 meetings and raising over £13,000. Never did he lose a moment's precious time on board. From London to Gibraltar he had already written 160 letters. From Gibraltar to Naples he edited the Aniwan translation of the *Shorter Catechism*. Two years previous, he had prepared the New Testament in the Aniwan language, a project completed mostly 'in trains—steadying the paper on the back of his hand, at junctions waiting for connections, in station waiting rooms'.

Sunset

By 1898, four decades after he first sailed to the New Hebrides, there were two-dozen missionaries and their wives ministering on the islands. Among them were two of his sons. Well into his seventies he continued to write Aniwan catechisms, hymns, and Scripture translations. At seventy-nine, he was still on Aniwa doing the Lord's service. 'I cannot visit the villages, or go among the people and the sick, as formerly, owing to an increased feebleness in my legs ... but it is all as our Master sends it, and we submit thankfully.'[9]

In 1904, John and Margaret enjoyed their fortieth wedding anniversary in the most lovely place they could imagine: the Aniwan Islands. It would be their last trip. On June 3, 1905, the world mourned the death of missionary titan, Hudson Taylor. Less known was the death of Margaret Paton a few days earlier on May 23.

In 1906 the Committee refused his request to return to the islands.

> I am exceedingly grieved at this, but fear I must submit. They say I am too old and frail to be allowed to go alone, and yet the evidence of my strength is that I can still address a meeting daily, and three on every Sabbath, but I shall still keep agitating until they let me go![10]

On January 28, 1907, at the ripe old age of eighty-two, John Paton was laid to rest in Melbourne, Australia, in the Boroondara cemetery. After decades of near misses and the worst dangers imaginable, the Lord put him to rest in *his* time. Paton's desire was granted, that he 'might be permitted of God to work to the very end'.

He had lived long enough to see the day when thousands of converts on the islands were singing the praises of their Saviour the Lord Jesus Christ. Like John G. Paton, many

---

[9] Ralph Bell, *John G. Paton: Apostle to the New Hebrides* (Butler: Highley Press, 1952), p. 238.

[10] Langridge and F. Paton, *Later Years and Farewell*, p. 226.

suffering believers wonder why God allows painful things to happen. Yet Paton's life in retrospect shows how God was employing these trials to prepare him for greater usefulness. Those who are forced to uproot prematurely may see in Paton one who diligently followed the hidden ways of God. 'God moves in a mysterious way', the poet has memorably said. The means God uses to displace and change may be painful, but never purposeless; traumatic, but never trifling; bitter, but always beneficial.

PART TWO

LESSONS FROM PATON'S LIFE

The Paton family circa 1887.

5

Paton's Godly Home

The outside world might not know, but we knew, whence came that happy light as of a newborn smile that always was dawning on my father's face. It was a reflection from the divine presence, in the consciousness of which he lived.[1]

—John G. Paton, observing his father's prayers

THOUGH godly fathers are rare, it should not be surprising that Paton had one. The agency foremost in sending him to the islands of the South Seas was not his church or missionary society but rather the godly home in which he was raised. From here a loving father set the footings of courage that would support a life of danger. From here the fervent prayers at mealtimes would shape his longing to bring salvation to the ends of the earth. From here the undying support of parents sustained him when others were coaxing him to stay. From here the hushed tones of family worship caused his heart to throb for Christ.

[1] Paton, *Autobiography*, p. 8.

A consecrated father

Paton's working-class father was filled to the brim with masculine instruction and tender oversight. He invested deeply in the emotional lives of his children. He did not shrink from physical affection or from weeping in their presence. When John was 'launched upon the ocean of life' to attend seminary, his father walked with him for the first six miles in tears and almost unbroken silence. The father gripped his boy: 'God bless you, my son! Your father's God prosper you, and keep you from all evil!' After embracing, Paton ran off, ascended a hill, and then recounts the memorable parting:

> I watched through blinding tears, till his form faded from my gaze; and then, hastening on my way, vowed deeply and oft, by the help of God, to live and act so as never to grieve or dishonour such a father and mother as he had given me. The appearance of my father, when we parted—his advice, prayers, and tears—the road, the dyke, the climbing up on it and then walking away, head uncovered—have often, often, all through life, risen vividly before my mind, and do so now while I am writing, as if it had been but an hour ago.[2]

This godly example was so formative that—even writing years later as an aged man—Paton could not forget his youthful longing to follow Jesus and hate sin because this is what his father desired.

[2] *Ibid.*, pp. 25-26.

In my earlier years particularly, when exposed to many temptations, his parting form rose before me as that of a guardian angel. It is no Pharisaism, but deep gratitude, which makes me here testify that the memory of that scene not only helped, by God's grace, to keep me pure from the prevailing sins, but also stimulated me in all my studies, that I might not fall short of his hopes, and in all my Christian duties, that I might faithfully follow his shining example.[3]

The significance of these words is tremendous. What was the instrument God used to keep Paton free from sin, sharp in study, and vigilant in sanctification during his years on the New Hebrides? It was his father's 'shining example'. As Scripture reveals ('Be imitators of me, as I am of Christ' [1 Cor. 11:1]), children learn most from what they *see*.

John's brother wrote a poem of tribute for his father, saying:

> The God-glow on his face attracted men,
> and children gazed and smiled,
> as if again Christ's eyes were on them bursting!

If this sounds like hyperbole, remember that even Stephen's killers could see his face aglow.

Fervent prayers

The source of Paton's stirrings for the unconverted world can be traced to his godly home. As a boy, he vividly recalled his father's intercessions at evening time:

[3] *Ibid.*

How much my father's prayers at this time impressed me I can never explain, nor could any stranger understand. When, on his knees and all of us kneeling around him in family worship, he poured out his whole soul with tears for the conversion of the heathen world to the service of Jesus, and for every personal and domestic need, we all felt as if in the presence of the living Saviour, and learned to know and love him as our divine friend.[4]

Paton's father would enter a little room for prayer after each meal. The children learned by a kind of 'spiritual instinct' that intercessions of the most holy nature were being offered up for them before the Great High Priest. 'We occasionally heard the pathetic echoes of a trembling voice pleading as if for life, and we learned to slip out and in past the door on tiptoe, not to disturb the holy colloquy.'

Teaching his sons how to pray was the greatest gift the senior Paton gave to missions. Years later Paton would dig a well on Aniwa that saved the lives of all the inhabitants. The natives later tried to sink a half-dozen wells in the most likely places but failed each time. The explanation could only be Paton's Godward petitions. A native said: 'Missi not only used pick and spade, but he prayed and cried to his God. We have learned to dig, but not how to pray, and therefore Jehovah will not give us the rain from below!'

[4] *Ibid.*, p. 21.

Undying support

Living in an era of widespread poverty and being the eldest of eleven children, Paton would have been expected to find gainful employment to support the rest of the family. Ministry overseas was out of the question.

Such was not the case in the Paton home. When Paton consecrated himself to missions, nearly everyone was opposed, that is, except his parents.[5] 'My dear father and mother, however, when I consulted them, characteristically replied that they had long since given me away to the Lord, and in this matter also would leave me to God's disposal.' He said, 'characteristically', because in the home where he grew up, approval for the work of the Great Commission was never an anomaly. Even though Timothy's unbelieving father played no role in his son's future calling, he succeeded as a missionary because his spiritual father took such great pains to shape and support him. As the apostle Paul was the spiritual father and chief advocate for Timothy's ventures, so was Paton's father his primary champion and supporter.

The reader may gain a greater appreciation for Paton's sympathetic home and familial support by observing the life of Robert Nesbit, another Scottish missionary who entered overseas missions decades earlier. In the 1820s, six students at the University of St Andrews (Scotland's oldest school of

---

[5] Contrast this with the family of William Carey. When he had undertaken to sail to India as a missionary, he faced the serious predicament of a wife who resisted and rebelled and a father who thought his son's decision, 'the folly of one mad'. S. Pearce Carey, *William Carey* (1923; repr., London: Wakeman Trust, 2008), pp. 99-101.

learning), and their teacher Thomas Chalmers, became so enthralled with foreign evangelism that some consider the St Andrews Seven to be the finest flowering of missionary zeal in Scottish history. While each began making plans for mission-ary service in India, Robert Nesbit was finding considerable resistance from his mother. One author observed: 'No parent ever opposed a son's missionary ambition as inveterately as the mother of Robert Nesbit.'[6] She was painfully close to her son, to the point of smothering him. She devised every excuse imaginable to convince him to stay, even calling him a hopeless preacher whom the Indian people would find quite impossible. Nesbit did eventually reach Calcutta, even noting the benefit this struggle had in aiding new converts whose parents would cling to their children. Nonetheless, Nesbit's move to the mission field came with much emotional strain, something Paton happily avoided.[7]

Family worship

Every day, the Paton home played out the drama of Proverbs 4:1: 'Hear, O sons, a father's instruction, and be attentive, that you may gain insight.' Paton spoke with fondest memories of

[6] Stuart Piggin and John Roxborogh, *The St Andrews Seven* (Edinburgh: Banner of Truth Trust, 1985).

[7] Piggin and Roxborogh, *St Andrews Seven,* pp. 99, 110. Alexander Duff's father also had great difficulty parting with his brilliant son. Duff wrote to his father: 'Will you be a loser by so giving me up to the Lord, and so praising him for his goodness in having called me to so mighty a work? No, God will bless you with the blessing of Abraham, will enrich you with his faith, and will reward you a thousand-fold for your willing resignation and cheerful readiness in obeying God's command.'

family worship in the home, where father would take down the large family Bible, lead his children in a metrical psalm, read a passage of Scripture, discuss the implications, then close with prayer.

> Never, in temple or cathedral, on mountain or in glen, can I hope to feel that the Lord God is more near, more visibly walking and talking with men, than under that humble cottage roof of thatch and oaken wood. Though everything else in religion were by some unthinkable catastrophe to be swept out of memory, or blotted from my understanding, my soul would wander back to those early scenes, and shut itself up once again in the Sanctuary Closet, and, hearing still the echoes of those cries to God, would hurl back all doubt with the victorious appeal, 'He walked with God, why may not I?'[8]

A great preacher has remarked that some men accomplish much more by those whom they teach than by their own personal labours.[9] These early years of sincere family worship were not lost upon young John Paton. Little did his father know that by training his son he would be training islands of cannibals.

On Aniwa, one of the first steps in Christian discipline for new converts was family worship every morning and evening. 'Doubtless the prayers [of the natives] were often very queer, and mixed up with many remaining superstitions; but they

---

[8] Paton, *Autobiography*, p. 8.

[9] James M. Garretson, *Princeton and Preaching: Archibald Alexander and the Christian Ministry* (Edinburgh: Banner of Truth Trust, 2005), p. 29.

were prayers to the great Jehovah, the compassionate Father, the Invisible One—no longer to gods of stone!'[10]

Paton's gospel changed the role the father played in the home. It also increased the place of honour the Aniwan wives would now enjoy.

> In the old heathenism a woman had no part in the religious life of the community. She was a mere slave without a soul, except a slave's soul, which was liberated by the strangling of her body on the death of her husband—liberated only to continue as a slave in the spirit world. Now, the wife and mother is the centre of the house, honoured and reverenced as she is only where the spirit of Jesus has entered.[11]

Religious instruction was taught *outside* the home as well. Paton wrote about how the family's Sunday-morning walks home from church were lively with discussion about the sermon. The Patons' Christianity was real and authentic.

> There were eleven of us brought up in a home like that; and never one of the eleven, boy or girl, man or woman, has been heard, or ever will be heard, saying that Sabbath was dull or wearisome for us. But God help the homes where these things are done by force and not by love![12]

Hard work

As a boy, John learned to work hard. In the midst of his toil, he never lost track of why he was working, or for whom.

---

[10] Paton, *Autobiography*, p. 356.
[11] F. Paton, *The Kingdom in the Pacific*, p. 103.
[12] *Ibid.*, p. 17.

> We wrought from six in the morning till ten at night, with an hour at dinner-time and half an hour at breakfast and again at supper. These spare moments every day I devoutly spent on my books, chiefly in the rudiments of Latin and Greek; for I had given my soul to God, and was resolved to aim at being a missionary of the cross, or a minister of the gospel. Yet I gladly testify that what I learned of the stocking frame was not thrown away. The facility of using tools, and of watching and keeping the machinery in order, came to be of great value to me in the foreign mission field.[13]

This work ethic carried him through all of his years and travels. While in his seventies, he criss-crossed the globe, speaking to thousands, sometimes in as many as ten meetings weekly and five meetings on a Sunday. That which spurred him on was the exhilaration that comes from hard work! 'My only stimulant was the ever springing fountain of pure joy in the work of my Lord and Saviour Jesus Christ!'

Paton: the product of a godly father

Unlike the man who buried his money in the ground, Paton sought to multiply the influence of a godly home by teaching and modelling the righteous atmosphere in which his parents raised him. To have spurned such a heritage overtly, or even to have belittled it by minimizing the home's importance, would have been to Paton among the most heinous of sins.

For those of us privileged with parents akin to Paton's, we must never forget the demands that God has laid upon

[13] Paton, *Autobiography*, p. 21.

us. Paton was not content with believing children only, but desired that God would turn all hearts toward earnest devotion to Christ. Of all the titles Paton would have been happy to use, 'father' was most certainly top of the list, for in that role he not only looked forward to the future of his children but backward to the legacy of his forbears. Guides may shame, fathers bless. Authoritarians may berate, fathers nurture. Teachers scold, fathers admonish. Disciplinarians are current, fathers are timeless.

Many have not been blessed to grow up in such a home. The sense of loss—the sins and heartache that could have been avoided had home life been different—often brings despair. But each person can determine from the present time to craft a home as Paton's father did. By forgetting what is behind, the future is bright for those who choose to build their children's lives upon the sure promises of God's word. If God can reshape an island of cannibals into the image of Jesus Christ through the transformation of the home, may he not also do it in 'civilized' societies?

6

Paton's Clear Calling

Scotch Presbyterianism has produced three unsurpassed heroes of foreign missions—Alexander Duff, David Livingstone, and John G. Paton. They all belonged to the old granite formation, and were all lineal descendants of the Covenanters.[1]

—Theodore L. Cuyler

WHEN two years of appeals for South Sea missionaries failed, John Paton's Scottish denomination resolved to cast lots to determine if a minister from home should be sent overseas. The congregation sat in hushed silence as the elders examined the paper votes. The results were indecisive. Their laps were full of lots but their hands empty of a verdict.

Meanwhile, Paton—though happy and successful in his Glasgow ministry—had become convinced that life among the cannibals was *his* lot. 'I returned to my lodging with a lighter heart than I had for some time enjoyed, feeling that nothing so clears the vision, and lifts up the life, as a

[1] Langridge and Paton, *Later Years and Farewell*, p. 40.

decision to move forward in what you know to be entirely the will of the Lord.'

When it seemed nothing could spur the church toward missions on the New Hebrides, what was it that stirred the heart of Paton? What pushed and propelled and prompted him to preach and plead and plod? More broadly, why do missionaries do what they do?

A summary of motives

In 1956, Johannes Van den Berg wrote a book identifying ten major motives of the missionary awakening in Great Britain in the eighteenth century. They were: (1) politics, (2) humanitarianism, (3) asceticism, (4) guilt, (5) romance, (6) God's glory, (7) love, (8) the church, (9) eschatology, and (10) Jesus' command.[2]

While some of these are more valid than others, it is clear the impetus for world missions is complex not simple. Correct motives in missions are vital, as they will lead to greater endurance and less discouragement. Conversely, wrong motives make single-term missionaries. A romantic feeling wears off quickly. What the foreign field is and what we thought it to be are rarely identical.

Upon his arrival on Tanna, Paton confessed:

> My first impressions drove me ... to the verge of utter dismay. On beholding these natives in their paint and

[2] Cited, Martin I. Klauber and Scott M. Manetsch, *The Great Commission: Evangelicals and the History of World Missions* (Nashville: Broadman & Holman, 2008), pp. 58-63.

nakedness and misery, my heart was as full of horror as of pity. Had I given up my much-beloved work and my dear people in Glasgow, with so many delightful associations, to consecrate my life to these degraded creatures?[3]

It took Paton all of one minute for the second-guessing to begin. Yet, he gave the rest of his life to these islanders. Among his chief motives was the destiny of the lost.

Damnation: a driving force

Lost souls were the visitors endlessly knocking upon Paton's conscience. He spoke often of 'the wail of the perishing heathen in the South Seas'. The claims of the cannibals sounded in his ears. Hell motivated him as it has legions of others throughout church history. The pioneer, Hudson Taylor, spoke to his listeners about the 'great Niagara of souls passing into the dark in China. Every day, every week, every month they are passing away!'[4]

But by the turn of the twentieth century, eternal damnation was far from, shall we say, the *dernier cri.* The judgment of God had lost its grip as a chief force behind missions. Scotland's capital hosted the World Missionary Conference in 1910, just three years after Paton's death. It was supposed to be a high water mark in the evangelization of the world. Instead, liberalism had taken root in the movement and the gathering was

---

[3] Paton, *Autobiography*, p. 66.

[4] Quoted, Paul A. Varg, 'Motives in Protestant Missions, 1890–1917', *Church History* 23, no. 1 (March 1954), p. 71.

a flop.[5] Missionary fervour is housed in the womb of divine retribution. Kill the mother and the baby dies.

Observing the conference from afar in Calabar, veteran missionary Mary Slessor was not surprised:

> Where are the men? Are there no heroes in the making among us? No hearts beating high with the enthusiasm of the gospel? Men smile nowadays at the old-fashioned idea of sin and hell and broken law and a perishing world, but these [ideas] made men, men of purpose, of power and achievement, and self-denying devotion to the highest ideals earth has known.[6]

The greatest evangelists of the New Testament preached Christ *because* of judgment, not in spite of it. The first recorded words of John the Baptist were 'flee from the wrath to come' (Luke 3:7). The first words of Paul's evangel: 'the wrath of God is revealed from heaven' (Rom. 1:18). The first action of the all-conquering, risen Lord Jesus as he bolts from heaven on a white steed: 'He will tread the winepress of the fury of the wrath of God the Almighty' (Rev. 19:15).

D. A. Carson is right: 'If we refuse to see what the Bible says about the wrath of God, we will certainly fail to see what the cross achieves.' Ignoring offensive portions of Scripture is

---

[5] 'While many were enthusiastic about the World Missionary Conference in Edinburgh (1910), others regarded it as "the apotheosis" of missionary triumphalism; for [Roland] Allen, the conference epitomized his worst misgivings about the current attitudes of Western missionaries.' Eckhard J. Schnabel, *Paul the Missionary* (Downers Grove: IVP, 2008), p. 11.

[6] Quoted, Murray, *Scottish Christian Heritage*, p. 225.

a refusal of the word of God, not an alternative hermeneutical technique to interpret it. Hell discarded on the scrap heap of evangelistic incentives is hell denied upon the clear reading of Scripture.

If our Lord was willing to use hell as an incentive to reject anger (Matt. 5:22), lust (Matt. 5:29-30), and hypocrisy (Matt. 23:15), it is not surprising that he also used hell to awaken thoughts about the sinner's eternal destiny (Matt. 10:28). John Piper warns if we do not feel the truth of hell, 'the gospel passes from *good* news to just news. The intensity of joy is blunted and the heart-spring of love is dried up.'[7]

Perdition outside of Christ is not a carrot missionaries use to coax their converts to the Celestial City. It is a lens through which we see the justice of God; the sinfulness of man, and the splendour of the cross is seen.

Sooner or later, those ashamed of the doctrine of hell will cower in compunction before the demands of the Great Commission. If we lose the doctrine of damnation, gone not only is a powerful stimulant for world evangelism but also the glory of the gospel itself. Carson concludes:

> If we turn away embarrassed from what the Bible teaches of God's wrath, we will never glimpse the glory of what the Bible says about God's love, supremely manifested in Christ Jesus.[8]

---

[7] John Piper, *Brothers, We Are Not Professionals: A Plea to Pastors for Radical Ministry* (Nashville: Broadman & Holman, 2013), p. 134.

[8] Klauber and Manetsch, *Great Commission*, p. 187.

Lack of labourers

More than hell motivated Paton. For him, a need *did* necessitate a call, at least in part. Few were caring for the cannibals abroad, while many were willing to take up his Glasgow post. He reasoned it would be easier to find replacements at home than volunteers abroad.

> I clearly saw that all at home had free access to the Bible and the means of grace, with gospel light shining all around them, while the poor heathen were perishing, without even the chance of knowing all God's love and mercy to men.[9]

It could be argued that Paton's focus on the paucity of labourers was, in fact, misguided. Every place has a need, does it not? But Paton was arguing for much more. It was not only gospel preachers that the New Hebrides lacked. No doubt Scotland needed these as well. But the heathen islands were bereft of *access*. A westerner who forsakes the Bible does so because of lack of interest, lack of funds, or lack of understanding. But a Tanna-man rejects the Scriptures because they do not *exist*. The levels of rejection are not the same. Simon Magus spurned the Holy Spirit by trying to buy divine power (Acts 8). The Ephesians shunned the Spirit because they didn't know there was such a thing (Acts 19:2).

Paton saw the difference. The islanders lacked even the possibility because no one would volunteer. Decades later, after the first conversions on Aniwa, he still talked about the dearth of workers:

[9] Paton, *Autobiography*, p. 56.

My heart was so full of joy that I could do little else but weep. Oh, I wonder, I *wonder*, when I see so many good ministers at home, crowding each other and treading on each other's heels, whether they would not part with all their home privileges, and go out to the heathen world and reap a joy like this.[10]

Parental approval

Many opposed Paton's departure. But the key players—the leader of the Missions Committee, Paton's roommate, and his parents—were overjoyed. In the face of so many negative voices, John Paton—thirty-two years of age and independent as a lion—still humbly laid the matter before his godly parents. Their reply shows how integral their support was toward his calling:

> We feared to bias you, but now we must tell you why we praise God for the decision to which you have been led. Your father's heart was set upon being a minister, but other claims forced him to give it up. When you were given to them, your father and mother laid you upon the altar, their firstborn, to be consecrated, if God saw fit, as a missionary of the cross; and it has been their constant prayer that you might be prepared, qualified, and led to this very decision; and we pray with all our heart that the Lord may accept your offering, long spare you, and give you many souls from the heathen world for your hire.[11]

[10] *Ibid.*, p. 376.
[11] *Ibid.*, p. 57.

Let every parent note the weight such wise counsel will have upon their children's lives. Let every parent who clutches jealously to kith and kin ponder these words of Paton's godly parents. Let them contemplate whether it be hypocrisy to sing 'Give of thy sons to bear the message glorious', but 'glorious' only if that son belongs to someone else. When it seemed the whole world of Christian influence impeded John's plans, it was the words of his parents that buttressed his resolve. Whatever uncertainty he may have had, it melted like snow atop the glowing hearth at home.

Not only had the counsel of parents played a key role in Paton's initial move toward missions but so did the advice of respected guides later on in his ministry. After fleeing Tanna, his original plan was to remain on Aneityum and translate the Scriptures into Tannese. But the other missionaries, including Joseph Copeland, urged him to visit the churches in Australia and tell them the needs of the mission on the islands. Paton submitted to this wisdom, which led him into one of the most productive ministries of his life.[12]

The matter of the 'call' to missions later surfaced in the lives of Paton's own children. It was his unapologetic goal that each of his children become missionaries.[13] When their fifth son was born in 1878, Margaret said her husband was 'in

[12] On another occasion, he was urged by his advisors to visit Britain to raise support even though he was against it. He again succumbed, but this time only after he had cast lots and the paper read 'Go home'.

[13] This objective Paton certainly met. The Paton family became a missionary dynasty of four generations in the New Hebrides. See the family tree in Appendix B below for more details.

the seventh heaven of gratification at having another "little missionary" to devote to "the noblest work on earth"'. For Paton, no calling was greater:

> Let me record my immovable conviction that this is the noblest service in which any human being can spend or be spent; and that, if God gave me back my life to be lived over again, I would without one quiver of hesitation lay it on the altar to Christ, that he might use it as before in similar ministries of love, especially amongst those who have never yet heard the name of Jesus. I deeply rejoice—when I breathe that prayer that it may please the blessed Lord to turn the hearts of all my children to the mission field; and that he may open up their way and make it their pride and joy to live and die in carrying Jesus and his gospel into the heart of the heathen world![14]

This perspective carried over to grandchildren as well. Well into his seventies, Paton still felt the weight of the Lord's 'hate his own family' commands (Luke 14:26).

> Rather than cut himself in any way adrift from his work, he debarred himself from one of the chief blessings of old age, the presence of his beloved children, and the special delight of being surrounded by little grandchildren, who loved him.[15]

Margaret Paton tried to balance her husband's zeal. It was incredibly difficult for her to part with her children. 'I've got

[14] *Ibid.*, p. 444.
[15] Langridge and Paton, *Later Years and Farewell*, p. 222.

heart disease ... only the sight of my bairns can cure it.' In her estimation, it is better to offer each child to the Lord and let him determine their life's work. 'He shall have them all for the mission field, if he calls them to it, for I know that in that case he will give me the necessary—well, I hardly like to come out with it, *resignation!*'

John groaned at the word 'resignation'. It seemed far too passive. Parents ought to *encourage* their children into missions, not simply allow them. But Margaret counters admirably:

> I find that those very noble women whom he holds up as examples to me, in devoting their sons from infancy to be missionaries, and whose only regret is that they have not another dozen to dedicate, *have never been in the mission field themselves.* I once met a lady whose only son, she told me with kindling eyes, had been dedicated to the mission field, and her greatest earthly wish was to see him ready to go. I looked at her with a respect amounting to awe; but the bump of reverence not being too largely developed, it soon gave way to curiosity as to what her ideas of the mission field really were. I found that she laboured under the impression that her boy had only to get on to a heathen island and hold up a Bible amongst an interesting group of Ethiopians, who with outstretched arms had been crying out in vain, 'Come over and help us!' Now, having been behind the scenes, and knowing what it actually costs, my dedication of them will be worth something when it comes![16]

[16] Margaret Paton, *Letters from the South Seas,* pp. 233-34.

Let the reader decide who was right. But husband and wife were united in that their children should never be discouraged from such a noble task and Christian parents must do all they can to prepare them for it.

Pastoral gifting

The church should have taken Paton's ability as a reason to send him. Sadly, like so many today, the church tried to use Paton's local success as an anchor to keep him at home. In doing this, it missed a special opportunity to follow the pattern of the church in Antioch.

The church in Antioch did not send out Paul and Barnabas haphazardly. They did not start their missionary careers during the 'first' journey in Acts, but may have had as many as fifteen and ten years' experience of missionary service respectively. Regarding their arrival in Antioch, Schnabel observes: 'Neither Barnabas nor Paul were missionary novices: they were experienced missionaries who had seen many people come to faith in Jesus Christ, both Jews and Gentiles, who had seen churches established, who had taught new believers, and who had seen churches grow.'[17]

Nonetheless, the church in Antioch did not send out Paul and Barnabas without careful thought, but watched them for a year before sending them out to the work they were called and equipped to do (Acts 13:1-3). Likewise, for years the parishioners and church leaders had opportunity to watch

[17] Schnabel, *Paul the Missionary*, p. 75.

Paton's ministerial gifts at work while he was a Glasgow City missionary. They could see his proclivity for the down-and-outs, a valuable virtue for overseas missions. 'On Glasgow's Skid Row he became acquainted with the other side of life—its seamy, filthy, and wretched side.'[18] Gospel success ought more often be the driving force for churches to send away, not stash away, its best servant-workers.

R. B. Kuiper and wrong motives

Paton realized not all motives for missions are good. He would have echoed the words of R. B. Kuiper, who warned Christians to be on their guard against entering missions for the halo or for the sense of adventure. Do not go, cautioned Kuiper, simply to avoid the onerous task of preaching to a higher culture. Nor should you imitate the man who, 'troubled by an inferiority complex in civilized [society], reckons that a sense of superiority over uncivilized Africans is a thing to be grasped'.[19]

Paton's calling was clear because the right things motivated him. The horrific depths of hell, the shocking dearth of workers, and the wise counsel of parents were matched only by the highest joy of all:

> My heart often says within itself—when, *when* will men's eyes at home be opened? When will the rich and the learned

---

[18] Bell, *Apostle to the New Hebrides*, p. 42.

[19] R. B. Kuiper, *God-Centred Evangelism* (London: Banner of Truth Trust, 1966), p. 96.

and the noble and even the princes of the earth renounce their shallow frivolities, and go to live amongst the poor, the ignorant, the outcast, and the lost, and write their eternal fame on the souls by them blessed and brought to the Saviour? Those who have tasted this highest joy, 'the joy of the Lord', will never again ask—*Is life worth living?*[20]

---

[20] Paton, *Autobiography*, p. 412.

The reception of the Rev. John Williams at Tanna in the South Seas,
on the day before he was massacred, 1839.

7

Paton's Undaunted Courage

> The evening and morning hymn of praise has for ever
> supplanted the death-wail that so often struck a thrill of
> horror through the village.[1]
>
> —Frank Paton

ONE theologian has observed that the most frequent
negative prohibition from the lips of the Lord Jesus is
'fear not!' Yet the Lord never taught that the way to avoid fear
was to muster up some kind of irrational courage.

> God doesn't simply command courage with no reason
> behind it. In nearly every incident where God says 'fear not',
> there follows a reason to have courage, and that reason is
> God himself, his nature and his perfect plans.[2]

Jesus consoled his disciples by giving a basis for overcoming
fear. 'Fear not … *for* it is your Father's good pleasure to give

---

[1] F. Paton, *Kingdom in the Pacific*, p. 98.

[2] R. C. Sproul, 'What Does the Bible Say About Courage?', www.ligonier.org,
accessed May 10, 2016.

you the kingdom' (Luke 12:32). Gabriel told Mary, 'Do not be afraid … *for* you have found favour with God' (Luke 1:30). Zechariah was reminded, 'Do not be afraid … *for* your prayer has been heard' (Luke 1:13).

Missionaries with pluck and a high view of God often go to fields that are perilous. Paton and his contemporaries are fine examples of courage in the face of danger, as his son would concur:

> History has no braver records than those of the pioneer missionaries of the cross in the South Seas. Their greatest peril was from the evil deeds of their own countrymen, who had been before them at various places. But the savage could never be won without constant risk of life, and men were always found who did not count their lives dear unto themselves. It was when they saw their companions fall that these men felt the iron enter their souls.[3]

Paton is a model of courage not only for the danger that surrounded him but for the reasoning he used to overcome it. Before addressing how Paton overcame fear and danger, it is important to establish two factors that added fuel to Europe's fear of missions to the South Pacific islands. The first was the death of John Williams; the second was the current literature depicting the lurid scenes of cannibalism. Without an understanding of these two items and the *milieu* in which Paton lived, one cannot fully appreciate the magnitude of his bravery.

[3] F. Paton, *Kingdom in the Pacific*, p. 49.

The martyrdom of John Williams

John Williams is sometimes called the 'Apostle of the South Seas' because of his ground-breaking missionary work in the Polynesian Islands. His later martyrdom made him modern Britain's first missionary hero.[4] He was a godly man of resolve, common sense, and remarkable resourcefulness. After eighteen years of ministry, and at the age of thirty-eight, he could claim that no island of importance within 2,000 miles of Tahiti had been left unvisited. After nearly two strenuous decades of service, he returned to England, published a spellbinding book, received high acclaim, and was hailed as the greatest missionary of his times.

And yet with all his fame, he still had not forgotten the islands of the New Hebrides. As far back as 1824, he had talked to his wife about starting a work there but put the matter on hold after she responded with sheer dread:

> How can you suppose that I can give my consent to such a strange proposition? You will be eighteen hundred miles away, six months absent, and among the most savage people we are acquainted with and if you should lose your life in the attempt, I shall be left a widow, with my fatherless children, twenty thousand miles from my friends and my home.[5]

Apparently time had either softened his wife or emboldened Williams. By November 1839 he was sailing straight for

---

[4] *Biographical Dictionary of Evangelicals*, eds. Timothy Larsen, David W. Bebbington, Mark A. Noll (IVP Academic, 2003), p. 737.

[5] John Campbell, *The Martyr of Erromanga: Labours, Death, and Character of the Late Rev. John Williams* (London: John Snow, 1842), p. 230.

Erromanga in the New Hebrides. He had an innate frustration with fields overloaded with missionaries and a perpetual restlessness to move toward untouched lands: 'A missionary was never designed by Jesus to get a congregation of a hundred or two natives and sit down at his ease as contented as if every sinner were converted, while thousands around him, and a few miles from him, are eating each other's flesh, and drinking each other's blood with a savage delight, living and dying without the knowledge of that gospel by which life and immortality are brought to light.'[6]

Because he could not content himself 'within the narrow limits of a single reef', sailing toward the New Hebrides was inevitable. Everyone knew that the reputation of these islands, including Tanna, was one of ill-mannered treatment of visitors. This should be expected. Some of the white traders were kind and upright, but many were malicious—often mistreating the natives—and the natives made no distinction between missionary and sailor. Both were white. One New Hebrides missionary observed:

> The evils committed by the white man on these shores, who can estimate? As we approach, we find them red with blood, spilt through the cupidity and avarice of the foreigners. The natives, after the first visit of the white man, know him only as a savage, and, standing at a distance, terrified at our approach, bid us begone from their shores; or, bent upon

[6] Richard Lovett, *History of the London Missionary Society: 1795–1895* (London: H. Frowde, 1899), I:256.

revenge, they allow us to come nigh, and devise a thousand schemes to ensnare us as their victims.[7]

But this was not enough to dissuade Williams. Having left his family on a nearby island some time earlier, he set out for what would be his last voyage. As his ship neared Erromanga, he penned his last entry in his journal on November 18, 1839: 'This is a memorable day, a day which will be transmitted to posterity, and the record of events which have this day transpired will exist after those who have taken an active part in them have retired into the shades of oblivion and the results of this day will be …'[8] The sentence is unfinished. Did Williams have a premonition of his own death?

Flanked by three other Europeans in a small rowing-boat, Williams approached the shore slowly. The empty beach was ominous. All was quiet as they marched up the shore and into the thicket. Then came the unexpected. 'Suddenly, without provocation, the attack came. Williams had time to turn and make a dash for the beach, but he was clubbed to death as he tried to out-swim his assailants. One of the missionaries made it safely to the boat. Unable to go ashore to recover the bodies, [the Captain] sailed for Sydney to secure help. Two months later they returned, and after negotiating with the natives, were given the bones of Williams and his comrade, the flesh of which had been eaten by the natives.'[9]

[7] Patterson, *Missionary Life Among the Cannibals*, p. 154.

[8] John Gutch, *Beyond the Reefs: The Life of John Williams, Missionary* (London: Macdonald and Company, 1974), p. 148. The reasons for Williams' murder are disputed. Some say previous visitors that day instigated the natives to seek revenge.

[9] Ruth Tucker, *From Jerusalem to Irian Jaya* (Grand Rapids: Zondervan, 1983), pp. 223-24.

Thus fell John Williams,[10] whose martyrdom earned him, as one missionary said, a 'niche in the temple of immortality'. Paton would write: 'Thus were the New Hebrides baptized with the blood of martyrs; and Christ thereby told the whole Christian world that he claimed these islands as his own. His cross must yet be lifted up, where the blood of his saints had been poured forth in his name! The poor heathen knew not that they had slain their best friends.'[11]

The literature of cannibalism

Daniel Defoe's *Robinson Crusoe* (1719) was a window through which Europe saw the heathen world. He was among the first novelists to address cannibalism and succeeded in showing there are few acts so universally repugnant as the devouring of human flesh. After years alone on the island, Crusoe confesses his fear: 'if I once came into their power, I should run a hazard more than a thousand to one of being killed, and perhaps being eaten; for I had heard that the people of the Caribbean coast were cannibals, or men-eaters.'[12]

Friday, Crusoe's servant, suggested anger was the reason some were eaten and some were not. In his comprehensive book on cannibalism in the South Seas, Paul Moon observes: 'There is a sort of common sense to this explanation.

---

[10] George Turner and Henry Nisbet followed after Williams to the New Hebrides and actually settled on Tanna, but fled for their lives after just a few months. They spent the next several years ministering in Samoa instead.

[11] Paton, *Autobiography*, p. 75.

[12] Daniel Defoe, *Robinson Crusoe* (London: T. Hughes, 1824) p. 108.

Cannibalism is not, evidently, simply an indiscriminate and murderous means of securing food, but instead is tied in with the arts of war. … It is a sort of revenge in the most extreme form: the vanquished actually disappear down the throats of the victors.'[13]

A century later, two of Herman Melville's novels (*Typee* and *Moby Dick*)—published when Paton was in his twenties—clashed somewhat with Defoe's conclusions that cannibalism was morally indefensible. He laboured to put a decent face on cannibalism by lampooning the practice: 'Better to sleep with a sober cannibal than a drunken Christian.' He then loosens the noose on cannibalism even more through a parody of Jesus' words, putting the ingestion of humans and geese livers on the same level: 'Cannibals? Who is not a cannibal? I tell you it will be more tolerable for the Fejee that salted down a lean missionary in his cellar against a coming famine; it will be more tolerable for that provident Fejee, I say, in the day of judgment, than for thee, civilized and enlightened gourmand, who nailest geese to the ground and feastest on their bloated livers in thy *pâté-de-foie-gras*.'[14]

[13] Paul Moon, *This Horrid Practice: The Myth and Reality of Traditional Maori Cannibalism* (New York: Penguin Books, 2008), p. 30. Incidentally, a missionary from my own field of service in Elim, South Africa, said a similar thing 130 years ago: 'This eating of people should not be attributed to a revolting taste for the flesh of warriors … [but] the inveterate belief that whoever tastes human flesh is invulnerable in battle. Of all medicines, this one is the most effective to repel the blows of the enemy and to give victory.' Allen Kirklady, *Capturing the Soul: The Vhavenda and the Missionaries, 1870–1900* (Meno Park: Protea Book House, 2005), p. 227.

[14] Herman Melville, *Moby Dick* (1851; repr. New York: Farrar, Straus, and Giroux, 1997), p. 299.

All of Melville's literary powers, however, could not make cannibalism civilized any more than it could cause Europe to empathize with it. It was, no doubt, the most repulsive attribute of heathen life. By Paton's day, nothing was more paralyzing than the thought of a life spent among the heathen of the South Seas.

Double jeopardy

That there was peril awaiting missionaries in the New Hebrides is undeniable. Danger was the pennant that flew above the islands. When Paton gave himself to missions there in 1857, one can imagine the opposition he received. Fresh was the memory of John Williams and his bones picked clean. So was the literature of the day that reminded Europeans in the most graphic terms that cannibals were not to be trifled with. They were hostile to outsiders, ate the people they despised, and did what they could to keep out foreigners. When strangers did come, they goaded them to leave by word and spear. One chief told Paton:

> Our fathers loved and worshipped whom you call the Devil, the Evil Spirit; and we are determined to do the same. Now, our people are determined to kill you, if you do not leave this island; for you are changing our customs and destroying our worship, and we hate the Jehovah Worship.[15]

On another occasion, Paton asked an Aniwan chief where a certain pile of human bones had come from. The chief said

[15] Paton, *Autobiography*, p. 116.

his people were not like Tanna-men. 'We don't eat the bones!' (There is always someone worse than one's own tribe!)

The threats upon Paton's life came from a dozen directions. Once, when he entered a hut to help the sick, an ailing chief pulled out a butcher's knife and held it to Paton's heart:

> I durst neither move nor speak, except that my heart kept praying to the Lord to spare me, or if my time was come to take me home to glory with himself. There passed a few moments of awful suspense. My sight went and came. Not a word had been spoken, except to Jesus; and then [the chief] wheeled the knife around, thrust it into the sugarcane leaf, and cried to me, 'Go, go quickly!' … I ran for my life a weary four miles till I reached the mission house, faint, yet praising God for such a deliverance.[16]

The chief soon died and his people strangled one of the wives and hanged the other. Witchcraft was common. Often Paton denied the witch doctors had any power over him. With love and mettle bursting through his veins he said: 'I challenge all your priests to unite and kill me by sorcery or *nahak*. If on Sabbath next I come again to your village in health, you will all admit that your gods have no power over me, and that I am protected by the true and living Jehovah God!'[17] When their plans failed, Paton succeeded in giving them the gospel.

Even Sunday morning worship brought him into jeopardy. For those pastors who think preaching before a post-modern

[16] *Ibid.*, p. 191.
[17] *Ibid.*, p. 141.

congregation is menacing, consider Paton's flock on Aniwa: 'Our earlier Sabbath services were sad affairs. Every man came armed … with his weapons of war at his side and bow and arrow, spear and tomahawk, club and musket … ready for action.' Among the greatest threats Paton faced was the sheer number of missionaries who had suffered death. While Paton could write well, he was also one of the few left to write at all.

Modern readers stand aghast that missionaries could endure such peril. But were the actions of Paton and his colleagues that much different from the earliest evangelists? Paul too was in constant danger and 'often near death'. A catalogue of his sufferings are listed in 2 Corinthians 11:23-27. The writer of Hebrews praises the heroes of faith who, upon torture, refused to escape death by denying their Saviour and securing their release (Heb. 11:35).

Now we must turn to answer the question: From where did Paton's courage come?

'Behold, I am with you always'

The first source of Paton's courage was his intimate walk with the Lord Jesus Christ. The devout are often the most daring. The confidence accompanying godly people is not like the swagger of a boy carrying a toy gun but more akin to the boldness of a marine aboard a battleship. The latter knows where his strength lies. The *righteous*, says Proverbs, are bold as a lion (Prov. 28:1). Paton was so close to his Saviour and so convinced of his abiding presence, that not even the worst of hairbreadth escapes could deter him. 'In Jesus I felt invulnerable and immortal, so long as I was doing his work. And I can truly say, that these were the moments when I felt my Saviour to be most truly and sensibly present, inspiring and empowering me.'

Some find confidence in books and learning; Paton found courage in 'being with Jesus'. He was not fooled like the Jews, who expressed shock that boldness could be displayed in the 'uneducated' (Acts 4:13). His resolve came from the knowledge that he was in lockstep with the plans of God. 'Had it not been for the assurance that I was engaged in his service, and that in every path of duty he would carry me through or dispose of me therein for his glory, I could never have undertaken either journey.'[18]

John Piper believes the intimate moments Paton had with the Lord were the deepest source of his joy and courage. 'I would dare to say that to share this experience and call others to enjoy it was the reason that he wrote the story of his life.'[19] For Paton to be able to walk through the 'valley of the shadow of death' he must dwell in the 'shadow of the Almighty'.

> It is the sober truth, and it comes back to me sweetly after twenty years, that I had my nearest and dearest glimpses of the face and smile of my blessed Lord in those dread moments when musket, club, or spear was being levelled

---

[18] *Ibid.*, p. 148.
[19] Piper, *John G. Paton*, pp. 27-28.

at my life. Oh the bliss of living and enduring, as seeing 'him who is invisible'![20]

The eminent Puritan Stephen Charnock argued the reason so many good men are overcome by fear of their enemies is because they have forgotten the omnipresence of God. 'If the presence of God be enough to strengthen against fear, then the prevailing of fear issues from our forgetfulness of it.'[21] Though the devil stands *by* us, he would say, God stands *in* us. 'Fear not, *for* I am with thee' (Isa. 43:5). Those who are deaf to threats and possess hearts like iron are those who believe the promise that the divine presence will be with them (Matt. 28:20).

> Without that abiding consciousness of the presence and power of my dear Lord and Saviour, nothing else in all the world could have preserved me from losing my reason and perishing miserably. In his words, 'Lo, I am with you alway, even unto the end of the world', became to me so real that it would not have startled me to behold him, as Stephen did, gazing down upon the scene. I felt his supporting power.[22]

Great courage is the feeble overcoming fear by faith, not the resourceful overcoming risk with resolve.

---

[20] Paton, *Autobiography*, p. 117.

[21] Stephen Charnock, *Works* (1864; repr. Edinburgh: Banner of Truth Trust, 2010), I:449.

[22] Paton, *Autobiography*, p. 117. For Paton, the omnipresence of Christ was a source of courage for the head *and* the heart. 'Oh that all my readers knew and felt this, as in those days and ever since I have felt that his promise is a reality, and that he is with his servants to support and bless them even unto the end of the world' (p. 164).

Why mothers run quickly

Paton's courage also sprang from a prayer life submissive to God's over-arching plan. He did not make demands of God but instead acknowledged God's prerogative to do as he pleased. 'Thy will be done' was the letterhead above all his prayers, even when kneeling before his would-be killers.

> I … assured them that I was not afraid to die, for at death my Saviour would take me to be with himself in heaven, and to be far happier than I had ever been on earth. I then lifted up my hands and eyes to the heavens, and prayed aloud for Jesus … either to protect me or to take me home to glory as he saw to be for the best.[23]

Paton and his disciples never gave God ultimatums in prayer, as so many Word-Faith proponents do today. Their courage and confidence mingled with the assurance that God would do what is best. These prayers for boldness rubbed off on Paton's faithful friend Abraham. When cannibals surrounded the two with levelled muskets, Abraham prayed: 'Make our hearts good and strong for thy cause, and take thou away all our fears. Make us two and all thy servants strong for thee and for thy worship; and if they kill us two, let us die together in thy good work, like thy servants Missi Gordon the man and Missi Gordon the woman.'[24]

Paton learned this kind of submissive prayer from his parents when he was a boy. When the potato crop failed in Scotland,

[23] *Ibid.*, p. 164.
[24] *Ibid.*, p. 171.

and the food had run out, Mrs Paton gathered her little brood around her and said: 'O my children, love your heavenly Father, tell him in faith and prayer all your needs, and he will supply your wants so far as it shall be for your good and his glory.' Only mothers with a deep confidence in the sovereign workings of God will declare to their children that the Lord will never give for their good at the expense of his glory.

When surrounded by spears and daggers, Paton prayed for help and was delivered. 'Did ever mother run more quickly to protect her crying child in danger's hour, than the Lord Jesus hastens to answer believing prayer and send help to his servants in his own good time and way, so far as it shall be for his glory and their good?'[25]

Chief among Paton's requests in prayer was not deliverance from peril but boldness to overcome it. Again and again he asked for the courage to withstand. This is exactly what the New Testament saints prayed for as well. 'Making supplication … for me, that words may be given to me in opening my mouth boldly to proclaim the mystery of the gospel' (Eph. 6:19).

When the enemies of Jesus threatened the early apostles with privation and death (Acts 4:17-18), one would expect prayers for protection and rescue, begging God for safety and security from harm. Instead, they prayed for more courage: 'Now, Lord, look upon their threats and grant to your servants to continue to speak your word with all boldness' (4:29). Boldness comes when Christians pray.

[25] *Ibid.*, p. 164.

Calvary before Pentecost

The final source of Paton's courage was the belief that God often uses the death of his saints to bring life to sinners. Courageous people know the casket of death for one may mean the cradle of life for another. As he struggled over the death of his wife and newborn, he found hope in God's providence to bring life out of death.

> I do not pretend to see through the mystery of such visitations, wherein God calls away the young, the promising, and those sorely needed for his service here; but this I do know and feel, that, in the light of such dispensations, it becomes us all to love and serve our blessed Lord Jesus so that we may be ready at his call for death and eternity.[26]

This is important because a key weapon Satan employs against God's servants is the fear of dying. If fear of death is the prison Satan uses to keep Christians from occupying treacherous but needy mission fields, then the cross is the key that releases them. Through death Jesus delivers 'all those who through fear of death were subject to lifelong slavery' (Heb. 2:14-15).

Paton knew his death would only advance the gospel. Going down with the ship for one may mean a seat in the lifeboat for another. While some lose heart, others gain confidence. He would have agreed with Samuel Zwemer's statement that the unoccupied fields of the world must have

---

[26] *Ibid.*, p. 85.

their Calvary before they can have their Pentecost. But until God willed otherwise, Paton was indestructible. When a deadly throng of cannibals encircled Paton and his comrade, he lifted up his heart in prayer to God. Peace overwhelmed him.

> I realized that I was immortal till my Master's work with me was done. The assurance came to me, as if a voice out of heaven had spoken, that not a musket would be fired to wound us, not a club prevail to strike us, not a spear leave the hand in which it was held vibrating to be thrown, not an arrow leave the bow, or a killing stone the fingers, without the permission of Jesus Christ.[27]

This is why Paul could say: 'With full courage now as always Christ will be honoured in my body, whether by life or by death (Phil. 1:20). God's servants are most courageous when life or death is a win-win.

---

[27] *Ibid.*, p. 207.

8

Paton's Pensive Risk

Life, humanly speaking, is perfectly safe here.
> —Margaret Paton, speaking of Aniwa

I F the apostle Paul spoke of being in danger 'every hour' (1 Cor. 15:30), so could John Paton. Daily he courted fatality. Each moment on Tanna was a struggle to sustain life. Ruth Tucker refers to his *Autobiography* as play-by-play coverage of cannibals clubbing missionaries. 'Mere survival was a constant mental and physical strain, and staying alive was itself an achievement worth noting.'[1]

When is risk justified?

The obvious question arises: Is Paton's life on Tanna an example of risk or recklessness? At what point does one move from valiant to rash, from courageous to unwise, from unafraid to foolhardy? The lion-heart is praiseworthy, the kamikaze is not, but the line that divides the two is not always clear.

[1] Tucker, *From Jerusalem to Irian Jaya*, p. 224.

Paton's contemporaries hotly debated the nature of risk within missions. On one side of the dispute were those in 'Camp Caution'. Though in Paton's time this group was not as concerned about health and safety as they are in the present day, they generally promoted security and personal wellbeing.[2] On the other side were those in 'Camp Courage', whose motto was 'Nothing ventured, nothing gained.'

Though Paton dwelt mostly with the latter, he spent time within both camps. By entering into the jaws of danger—and then sometimes being delivered from them—Paton would end up receiving friendly fire from both sides. From Camp Courage he was criticized for not risking enough. After four years on Tanna—having endured the loss of his wife and child, persistent bouts of ague and malaria, the death of half a dozen co-labourers, constant calls for his life and the forfeiture of all his worldly possessions—Paton narrowly and miraculously escaped from the island, a move he thereafter had to defend. One critic offered the following rebuke: 'You should not have left. You should have stood at the post of duty till you fell. It would have been to your honour, and

[2] An example of this can be seen during the period when Geddie was preparing to leave Canada for the South Pacific. His church urged him to leave behind his three little children, who were five years old and younger at the time. He refused. However, months before their departure, his two youngest daughters (Jane and Mary) died inexplicably of illness. Then, nearly two decades later in 1864, while in transit to Australia for their first furlough in 15 years, their little two-year-old boy Alexander died and was buried at sea. That three of his children died *away* from the dangers of the islands shows, in part, that the safety of comfortable surroundings ought not to be overstated.

better for the cause of the mission, had you been killed at the post of duty like the Gordons and others.'[3]

There were also those from the cautious camp who implied that he was at least in part responsible for the death of his family. Such accusations, while he was weighed down under the burden of the heaviest of sorrows, combined to push his sanity to the brink.

> Oh, the vain yet bitter regrets, that my dear wife had not been left on Aneityum till after the unhealthy rainy season! But no one advised this course; and she, high-spirited, full of buoyant hope, and afraid of being left behind me, or of me being left without her on Tanna, refused to allow the thing to be suggested. In our mutual inexperience, and with our hearts aglow for the work of our lives, we incurred this risk which should never have been incurred; and I only refer to the matter thus, in the hope that others may take warning.[4]

One can imagine those lonely nights, pacing, wondering: 'Does the guilt lie with me? Was the risk too great?' That Paton *may* have battled such doubts would not fairly tell the story about what we know he believed. He was not a novice that stumbled into missions. He weighed, he reasoned, he went. Just as the apostle Paul had a concentrated theology of risk, so too did John Paton. What did it look like?

---

[3] Paton, *Autobiography*, p. 223.
[4] *Ibid.*, p. 80.

Reality of risk: mission is dangerous

Among Mary Paton's last words were these: 'If I had the same thing to do over again, I would do it with far more pleasure, yes, with all my heart. Oh, no! I do not regret leaving home and friends.' She understood the level of danger. They knew the degree of risk it would take to reach an untouched people with the gospel. They took it. The world identifies this kind of decision-making as being frivolous and careless with life. Jesus calls it counting the cost.

Paul and Barnabas—the first missionaries of the early church—'risked their lives' for the name of Christ (Acts 15:26). They went to people who made inexhaustible efforts to kill them. The Jews in Damascus, for example, 'guarded the gates day and night' in their attempts to assassinate Paul.

But was Paul's risk 'necessary'? Yes, if we define necessary as those means required to effectively carry out God's commands. A good example is Paul's stoning at Lystra. True, the next day he did not climb aboard a soapbox in the public square and pick up the sermon where he had left off. He wisely left for Derbe—only to come right back to Lystra! What was the message on his return? 'Through many tribulations we must enter the kingdom of God' (Acts 14:22). Paul's theology of risk was not defined as freedom from danger. He knew the reality of missionary work. Pain and peril were part of the task.

Critics charged some of the South Seas Islands missionaries with imprudence, implying they could have escaped unharmed. But define 'escape'. Define 'could have'. Paul 'could have' escaped the pain in Jerusalem, but he deemed going there as necessary for the task of the Great Commission. He was ready for both the prison and the gallows. His chief concern was not preservation of life but propagation of the gospel. He said: 'I do not account my life of any value' (Acts 20:24).

John the Baptist 'could have' escaped his beheading had he not pressed the serious matter of the immorality of Herod's wife. I can hear the remarks: 'Did you have to mention *that*? You poured salt into the wound, John. Now you'll have to live (and die) with the consequences.'

To avoid all risk is to avoid the Christian life. The apostle John, himself no stranger to danger, wrote: 'We ought to lay down our lives for the brothers' (1 John 3:16). This verse is not a catchphrase for missions but a command every Christian must willingly follow. Simon Kistemaker affirms the risk factor by reminding Christians that when the honour of God's name and the advancement of his church demand that we love our brothers, 'we ought to show our love at all cost—even to the point of risking and losing our lives'.

Risk is the inescapable consequence of missionary work.

Reason for risk: gospel, not adventure or pride

Ego is a wrong motive for risk. After being caught in another perilous situation, Paton wrote: 'None of this had been brought on by selfish pleasure, or self-willed obstinacy, but in devotion to [God's] will and in doing his work.'

Faith is the root of pensive risk, presumption is the root of thoughtless chance. Presumption was the third and final temptation Satan brought to Jesus in the wilderness (Luke 4:9-12). The devil called for Jesus to 'throw himself down' so that the angels could swoop in for the rescue. But while it is true that God has promised to guard and protect his beloved—as Satan pointed out in his quotation of Psalm 91—he has only promised this within the framework of his will. Snake handlers and poison drinkers take ill-advised risks because they are *not* trusting God. They are tempting him.

Matthew Henry's comment on the parallel passage in Matthew 4 is helpful: 'If we expect that—because God ... has promised to keep us, we may [then] wilfully thrust ourselves into danger, and may expect the desired end without using the appointed means—this is presumption, this is tempting God.'[5]

Geddie warned of needless risk. When he angered the natives on Aneityum by inadvertently cutting down sacred trees, he sought to appease them. 'Missionaries among a heathen people ought as far as possible to guard against everything that would outrage their feelings. Our zeal in the cause of God must be tempered with prudence, or we are in danger of defeating our object in living among them. Natives may be drawn, but they can never be forced or driven.'[6]

---

[5] *Matthew Henry's Commentary on the Whole Bible: Complete and Unabridged in One Volume* (Peabody: Hendrickson, 1994).

[6] John Geddie, *Misi Gete*, ed. R. S. Miller (Launceston: Presbyterian Church of Tasmania, 1975), p. 36.

Paton risked all for the gospel's sake, not his own. Oh, how grateful the natives were for the dangerous steps these missionaries were willing to take for Christ and kingdom. One islander said: 'Had he stayed away from such danger, I would have remained heathen; but he came, and continued coming to teach us, till, by the grace of God, I was changed to what I am.'

Paul never risked out of ambition for adventure. He and others were always being 'given over to death *for Jesus' sake*' (2 Cor. 4:11). When the Sanhedrin demanded Peter and John leave off preaching, their answer rested on gospel grounds: 'We cannot but speak of what we have seen and heard' (Acts 4:20). The apostle's daring is noticeable in his fellow workers Prisca and Aquila as well. Paul commended his friends because they 'risked their necks' for his life (Rom. 16:4). He saluted Epaphroditus for willingly handing over his life and exposing himself to danger: 'He nearly died for the work of Christ, *risking his life* to complete what was lacking in your service to me' (Phil. 2:30). And perhaps most difficult of all, when Paul was forced to flee the dangers of Berea, he left behind his prized understudies to fight the hazards alone (Acts 17:14-15). Even when they later joined him, they were sent right back into the *fracas* with an important letter (1 Thess. 3:5).

Rescue from risk: God's prerogative

The apostle Paul was not averse to avoiding danger. Cornered on one occasion, he escaped in a basket lowered down a city wall (Acts 9:25). When the Corinthians slandered the Way, he simply withdrew from the synagogue (Acts 19:9). It was Paul who thought a Mediterranean voyage in winter carried too much risk (Acts 27:10). Puzzling indeed is the notion that Paton should not have left Tanna. Did Paul not do likewise in Antioch? When his countrymen thrust the gospel aside, he turned to the Gentiles (Acts 13:46). And when things became too hazardous, he played his Roman citizenship as a trump card (Acts 25:11). The apostle did not view dodging danger as the coward's way out.

In the same way, Paton fought the armchair critics in their comfortable homes who criticized the 'cautious' decisions of the missionaries. He opposed suffering merely for suffering's sake. He preferred wisdom to imprudence.

> Life is God's great gift, to be preserved for his uses, not thrown away.

> We took what care we could, and God the Lord did the rest; or rather he did all—for his wisdom guided us, and his power baffled them.

> Though I am by conviction a strong Calvinist, I am no fatalist. I held on while one gleam of hope remained. Escape for life was now the only path of duty.

> I regard it as a greater honour to live and to work for Jesus, than to be a self-made martyr.

There are at least two benefits in escaping danger. First, God in his providence often glorifies himself by delivering his children from the jaws of death. We see this when Paul's nephew providentially uncovered the plot of a band of determined Jews to kill Paul. God loves to fight for his children. Paton often spoke of the 'Invisible One' constraining his would-be killers, for it was risk that put God's protection on display. Paton boasted of being 'invulnerable beneath his invisible shield'.

Second, flight from danger is often the means by which God transfers his people to new fields of service. How else would Paton have experienced his fifteen years of fruitful endeavour on Aniwa had he not first fled the dangers of Tanna? Apart from Paul's lengthy stays in Corinth and Ephesus, 'there is no explicit evidence that Paul ever stopped his missionary work in a city on his own initiative in order to start a new project in unreached areas'.[7] When God transports his servants, it is often on the heels of a storm.

Paton had great concern for family. It is true that he took his wife and child to the dangerous island of Tanna, but so apprehensive was he for Mary's safety that he built their house before she came over from the other island, before ministry endeavours, and before all language study. And lest outside observers view Paton as unconcerned about family, the words of Margaret Paton herself may be of help.

In her letters to friends and family back home she presents the softer side of Paton and the steps they took to guard their home. She speaks very much like a protective mother,

---

[7] Schnabel, *Paul the Missionary*, p. 197.

insisting on keeping her 'bairns' separate from the native children, fencing off the house, keeping the gates locked and forbidding all visitors in the home on Sundays. When John Paton bristled at the latter, insisting they were on the island for the benefit of the people, Margaret retorted that Sunday afternoons are for family! It is important to understand, however, lest Margaret appear as a snobbish colonial, that this separation of her children on Sunday was for 'weighty reasons'. She needed time alone on Sundays because 'for six days I am their devoted servant of Christ', and in getting these quiet hours she was sensitive it should be 'without hurting their feelings'.[8]

Ships of God's grace

To neglect God's means of rescue is to neglect the rescue itself. Paton wrote: 'Only when we use every lawful and possible means for the preservation of our life … can we expect God to protect us, or have we the right to plead his precious promises.' When John Mathieson, his fellow missionary, became unhinged mentally by the trauma of events, he locked himself in a room and told his wife and Paton that he would not run to safety but would rather die on the island. Paton records:

> We tried to show him the inconsistency of praying to God to protect us or grant us means of escape, and then refusing to accept a rescue sent to us in our last extremity. We argued that it was surely better to live and work for Jesus

[8] Margaret Paton, *Letters from the South Seas*, pp. 99-100.

than to die as a self-made martyr, who, in God's sight, was guilty of self-murder.[9]

The means God often uses to liberate his children is prayer. If risk is the cry for ships of God's grace, then prayer is the rope that moors them to the shore of life. Answered prayer is the means by which God delivers his people from danger. Once a hoard of homicidal natives were marching toward Paton and his friends. The village was in unspeakable terror; all routes of escape were blocked. On the brink of eternity, the men knelt in prayer. What followed is what one author called 'one of the greatest incidents in Christian missions'.[10] While Paton was praying, the approaching warriors stopped as if obstructed by an invisible wall, and then turned back.

> We were on that day his trusting and defenceless children; would you not, had you been one of our circle, have joined with us in praising the Lord God for deliverance from the jaws of death? I know not why they turned back; but I have no doubt it was the doing of God to save our lives.[11]

One matter of great dispute was the martyrdom of George and Ellen Gordon on Erromanga.[12] In 1861, the natives

---

[9] Paton, *Autobiography*, p. 171.

[10] Bell, *Apostle to the New Hebrides*, p. 130.

[11] Paton, *Autobiography*, p. 197.

[12] The death of John Williams on the island of Erromanga decades earlier has also caused some to imply at least partial guilt on his behalf due to his lack of caution. See Gutch, *Beyond the Reefs*, p. 156. Campbell argues, however, that while a spirit of adventure was among his greatest moral qualities, Williams' courage was balanced with other virtues. 'Yet with all his courage, he was far from being rash. Prudence regulated every movement of his life; and, until the fatal hour of his martyrdom on

wielding tomahawks hacked this dedicated couple to death, Ellen Gordon becoming the first female European martyr in the South Pacific. Earlier, an epidemic of measles swept through the islands, some think purposefully brought ashore by cruel white traders. On some islands, two-thirds of the population had been wiped out, the islanders so hot with fever they hollowed out ditches in the earth and covered themselves with soil. Many died in the graves they had just dug. The islanders were superstitious. They believed strongly in disease-makers, the universal impression being that Gordon was the cause. Could this misunderstanding have been avoided? Some argued, as did Geddie, that Gordon's imprudence of pronouncing temporal judgment upon the islanders and his 'dangerous experiment' of working without native teachers (who could have warned him) played a part in his death:

> His success was largely marred by his setting himself in opposition to the experiences of all the successful missionaries in the South Seas, especially in regard to the employment of natives as pioneers and helpers. Instead of regarding them as necessary for the opening up of a field, with his chivalrous courage, he declared himself ready to go where a native could go. And in carrying on his work, on account of their limited attainments, which had always been admitted, he tried to do without their aid.[13]

the ruthless shores of Erromanga, we see, upon all occasions, one uniform course of manly courage, combined with undeviating discretion.' Campbell, *Martyr of Erromanga*, p. 218.

[13] Patterson, *Missionary Life Among the Cannibals*, p. 449.

What was the conclusion? The risk was unnecessary. Those with this perspective could hardly be called cautious, for they were risking their lives on the islands as well. But while they honoured the Gordons for their service, they were also willing to critique unwarranted risk.

Paton, however, would have none of it. He was not incapable of biting sarcasm and he unleashed it in good measure against the Gordons' critics, especially those back home: 'Some severe criticisms, of course, were written and published by those angelic creatures who judge all things from their own safe and easy distance. George Gordon's lack of prudence was sorely blamed, forsooth! One would so like to see these people just for one week in such trying circumstances.'[14]

Perhaps he was loath to judge the Gordons because he had not forgotten the harsh words that came his way after his escape from Tanna. Some missionaries said he had taken 'too dark a view' of things and implied he was partly to blame for any future difficulties on the island. As one missionary put it: '[Paton's] removal for a time was necessary, but, to the regret of the other missionaries, he also removed the Aneiteumese teachers, thus breaking up the station altogether, although the friendly chiefs wished them to remain, and they were willing to do so. Abandoning the field altogether greatly increased the difficulty of resuming operations afterward.'[15]

Sometimes it behoves wise counsellors to warn against unwarranted risk. The apostolic church knew Paul's courage

[14] Paton, *Autobiography*, p. 167.
[15] Patterson, *Missionary Life Among the Cannibals*, p. 458.

and propensity for danger. They wisely shielded him from harm by sending him away to Tarsus (Acts 9:30) and later forbade him addressing the rioters in Ephesus (Acts 19:30). When Paton wanted to return to Tanna with his second wife, the missionary society determined he should instead go to Aniwa. It was the right decision.

Paton: risk for the sake of Jesus

Paton understood the reality of ministry on pioneer fields was risky and dangerous. But he also gives helpful guidance to those who do not serve in such places, for to avoid missions *because* of threat would be one step removed from the experience of real Christianity. Have we forgotten those bygone eras (and those that still exist today!) where simply becoming a Christian meant risking all? And what of the apostolic (indeed, dominical) pattern of fruitful service, expressed in Paul's words to the Corinthians: 'For we who live are always being given over to death for Jesus' sake, so that the life of Jesus also may be manifested in our mortal flesh. So death is at work in us, but life in you' (2 Cor. 4:11-12; cf. John 12:24-26).

Paton also reminds the church that risk ought always be for the purpose of Christ and his church, not conceit or excitement. As he let down his anchor in the midst of uncertainty, Paton was not averse to using means for securing his and his family's safety. Did he trust God? Yes, along with native bodyguards, guard dogs, and a musket.[16] Paton often used

---

[16] While Paton had a gun, he never intended to use it. 'The thought of [the firearms] did not enter our souls even in that awful time. I had gone to save, and not

any legitimate means he could to escape, ranging from the threat of divine judgment upon those who would harm him to brandishing an unloaded revolver beneath their noses. He knew that among the heroes of faith commended in the eleventh chapter of Hebrews were not only martyrs but also those who 'escaped the edge of the sword' (Heb. 11:34).

---

to destroy. It would be easier for me at any time to die, than to kill one of them. Our safety lay in our appeal to that blessed Lord who had placed us there, and to whom all power had been given in heaven and on earth.' Paton, *Autobiography*, p. 139. This is similar to the position of Jim Elliot and his fellow missionary martyrs to the Auca Indians in Ecuador, who refused to use guns to defend themselves.

Top: The church of Aniwa.
Bottom: The chief and teachers of Aniwa.

9

Paton's Gospel Strategies

In claiming Aniwa for Christ, and winning it as a small jewel for his crown, we had the experience which has ever marked God's path through history—he raised up around us and wonderfully endowed men to carry forward his own blessed work.[1]

—John G. Paton

D ID the apostle Paul have a missionary strategy? Yes and no. If by strategy is meant a deliberate, well-formulated, duly executed plan of action based on human observation and experience, then Paul had little or no strategy; but if we take the word to mean a flexible *modus operandi* developed under the guidance of the Holy Spirit and subject to his direction and control, then Paul did have a strategy.[2]

[1] Paton, *Autobiography*, p. 391, in partial reference to Namakei, the old chief of Aniwa, whose heart slowly but steadily opened to the light of the gospel.

[2] J. Herbert Kane, *Christian Missions in Biblical Perspective* (Grand Rapids: Baker, 1976), p. 76. Ekhard Schnabel argues that the missionary method of the early church focused on the faithful preaching of Christ and his gospel to whomever would listen and trust in the Holy Spirit to do the work. 'The geographical scope of Paul's missionary work was not controlled by a "grand strategy" that helped him decide in which cities to begin a new missionary initiative.' Schnabel, *Paul the Missionary*, p. 287.

Paton certainly would have agreed. He had given his life to the islands for one reason: preaching the gospel of Jesus. If evangelism was the summit, four paths ascended toward this goal: language study, church planting, financial aid, and social reform.

Learning the language

When Paton and his wife first arrived on Tanna, they knew nothing of the language. There was no Rosetta Stone, no language immersion class, no books in Tannese, no alphabet. John Geddie spoke of the 'drudgery' of moulding an unwritten language into letters and fixed sounds.[3] The missionary of ordinary and common disposition would never have come. Paton, however, was both extraordinary and uncommon. From the very beginning he jumped into the language with vigour. 'We eagerly tried to pick up every word of their language, that we might, in their own tongue, unfold to them the knowledge of the true God and of salvation from all these sins through Jesus Christ.'

Among the many difficulties the South Seas missionaries faced, Frank Paton listed language study as among the greatest. 'No one can penetrate very deeply into the minds and hearts of the people till he has learned to speak to them in their own mother tongue. A missionary is incapable of knowing the thoughts, ambitions and deepest throbbing of the native heart without first knowing his manner of speech.'

[3] Patterson, *Missionary Life Among the Cannibals*, pp. 61-62.

One might ask: 'Why can't the missionary just teach the natives English?' The missionaries were ready with an answer. 'For the same reason that a Chinese who came to persuade us to become followers of Confucius would have to learn our language. We don't want to become Confucianists, and we certainly should not be willing to learn a new and difficult language like Chinese just to give our visitors a chance to win us over.'[4]

Paton's humorous story of the 'talking wood' highlights the language's primitive nature. While building one day and needing some tools, Paton scribbled a few words on a plank of wood. He asked the chief to deliver it to Mrs Paton: 'The wood will tell her', he explained. This left the chief dumbfounded that a piece of lumber could ever speak. Sure enough, Mrs Paton looked at the wood and handed over the necessary items. The chief returned to Paton more confused than ever. Paton then sat down and explained. 'In broken Tannese I read to him the words, and informed him that in the same way, God spoke to us through his book.' When the Bible was finally translated many years later, the natives found that 'the miracle of a speaking page was no less wonderful than that of speaking wood!'

Language study was slow and difficult. Most of the languages spoken on the islands were different and sometimes this was also the case on a single island. Paton acquired the native tongue by learning two simple questions: 'What is

---

[4] F. Paton, *Kingdom in the Pacific*, p. 59.

your name?' and 'What is this?' When new missionaries came, he taught them by giving them a dozen or so words to memorize each day.

It would be difficult for modern readers—blessed with a dozen Bibles translations—to appreciate the thrill Paton must have felt when the first words of Scripture rolled through the makeshift press he had assembled on the island. Well past midnight and frustrated after many failed attempts, Paton finally held in his hands a portion of the word of God in Tannese. Beneath the pall of the moon as the island slept, he could not contain his joy:

> I literally pitched my hat into the air, and danced like a schoolboy round and round that printing press; till I began to think, Am I losing my reason? Would it not be liker a missionary to be upon my knees, adoring God for this first portion of his blessed word ever printed in this new language? Friend, bear with me, and believe me—that was as true worship as ever was David's dancing before the Ark of his God![5]

By immersing himself in Tannese, Paton was following the paradigm of 1 Corinthians 14—the communication of Scripture ought to be intelligible to all. This means, in the most fundamental sense, that faithful missionaries 'are willing to learn the language of the people to whom they want to preach the gospel, even if this takes years of hard work, rather

[5] Paton, *Autobiography*, p. 124.

than speaking through a translator'.[6] Frank Paton called the missionary's task of Scripture translation 'the most difficult and the most fruitful service he can render; without it no mission work can be deep or permanent'.

Fluency in Greek had earned Paul a platform before a Jewish mob; but fluency in Hebrew won their silence. In the same way, the acquisition of the native language served as a bridge to bring together men from cultures separated by half the globe. While Paton learned the dialect, so did his children. Frank would later say: 'The gospel comes nearer to them when spoken in their own familiar idiom, and it touches the inner springs of their being.'

In fact, Paton had become so entrenched in the language that he began to think in the native tongue. On one occasion, while speaking at a conference in Australia, he stopped abruptly just a few words into his closing benediction because his hold on English suddenly escaped him. Embarrassed, he finally gasped out an 'Amen', fearing that a sudden onslaught of foreign tongues from the pulpit would push the congregation into laughter.

Paton's remarkable story of how he discovered the term 'faith' in the Aniwan language is a window into the trials and joys missionaries face in language study. For many years the work of Bible translation was paralyzed because no equivalent could be found for such a significant theological word. The natives regarded 'to hear' as a comparable meaning for 'to

[6] Schnabel, *Paul the Missionary*, p. 378.

believe'. Not only was such an idea insufficient but it also made verses such as Romans 10:17—'faith comes by hearing'—impossible to translate. One day, as Paton was in his study chair, he asked one of the ladies passing by: 'What am I doing?' 'You're sitting down', she said. Paton then lifted his legs, rested his feet on the cross bar of the chair, leaned back and asked again: 'Now what am I doing?' '*Fakarongrongo*. You are leaning *wholly*. You have lifted yourself from every other support.'

Paton was elated. He had found his word. 'To "lean on" Jesus wholly and only is surely the true meaning of appropriating or saving faith. And now "*Fakarongrongo Iesu ea anea mouri*" ("Leaning on Jesus unto eternal life" …) is the happy experience of those Christian islanders, as it is of all who thus cast themselves unreservedly on the Saviour of the world for salvation.'[7]

Church planting strategies

No one could wrench the book of Acts and the demands of Christ from the centre of Paton's creed. He was there to plant churches and proclaim the news that Christ had redeemed a people from every tribe. To win these people would mean (primarily) the conveying of salvation, not civilization. But how? Paton was far from ambivalent.

> Plant down your forces in the heart of one tribe or race where the same language is spoken. Work solidly from the

[7] Langridge and F. Paton, *Later Years and Farewell*, p. 56.

centre, building up with patient teaching and life-long care a church that will endure. Rest not till every people and language and nation has such a Christ centre throbbing in its midst with the pulses of the new life at full play. Rush not from land to land, from people to people in a breathless fruitless mission. The consecrated common sense that builds for eternity will receive the fullest approval of God in time.[8]

Until the World Missionary Conference in Edinburgh in 1910, the goal of missions had been individual conversions, church planting, and social transformation through three main types of actions: evangelism, education, and medicine.[9] Paton did not gather congregations; he planted churches. Social ministry had its place but only as a handmaid to the Great Commission.

We plant down our European missionary with his staff at a given station. We surround him with native teachers, who pioneer amongst all the villages with outreach. His lifework is to win that island, or that people, for God and civilization. He masters their language, and reduces it to writing. He translates and prints portions of the Bible. He opens schools, and begins teaching the whole population. He opens a communicants' class, and trains his most hopeful converts for full membership in the church. And there he holds the fort, and toils, and prays, till the gospel of Jesus had not only been preached to every creature whom he can

[8] Paton, *Autobiography*, p. 496.
[9] Ralph D. Winter and Steven C. Hawthorne, *Perspectives on the World Christian Movement: A Reader*, 4th ed. (Pasadena, CA: William Carey Library, 2009), p. 236.

reach, but also reduced to practice in the new habits and the new religious and social life of the community.[10]

The missionaries met the challenge of receiving converts into church membership with great patience, trying not to make the door of admission too narrow nor too wide. Even when Geddie spoke of twelve hundred in Sunday attendance—but only sixty in membership—the standard remained a basic gospel testimony and evidence of a changed heart. 'When too much is required of converts from heathenism before they are brought into the fold of Christ, there is a danger of discouragement and apathy; and, on the other hand, to admit persons too freely must injure the character of Christianity.'[11]

Not until 1879 did the Synod agree upon eight questions that prospective church members should agree upon:

1. Do you believe that Jehovah is the only true God?

2. Do you believe that in the only true God there are three persons, namely Jehovah the Father, Jesus Christ the Son, and the Holy Spirit?

3. Do you believe that the Bible is the word of God?

4. Do you believe that you are a sinner in the sight of God, and unable to save yourself?

5. Do you believe that Jesus Christ came into the world and died in order to save us from our sins, and now lives in heaven to bless us?

[10] Paton, *Autobiography*, p. 495.
[11] Patterson, *Missionary Life Among the Cannibals*, p. 397.

6. Do you believe that the Holy Spirit alone by means of the truth enlightens and sanctifies the heart?

7. Do you resolve that you will now give up the service of Satan, and all bad conduct, and serve Jesus only?

8. Do you acknowledge it to be your duty to train up your children in the fear of the Lord, and to seek to bring others to the Saviour?[12]

Establishing strong indigenous leadership was a constant challenge. Even when the locals are theologically trained, the missionaries must avoid the extremes of transferring large responsibility *too soon* with keeping the work under foreign leadership for *too long*. Frank Paton suggests his father saw the latter as the error most common with missionaries.

> [Extended missionary rule] has been our tendency in the past, but the time has come for a cautious and tactful advance along the line of developing the power of initiative among the native leaders, and this can be done only by giving more and more of the direct supervision into their hands. No doubt they will make many and foolish mistakes at first, but only thus can they learn, and only thus can a strong and independent native church be developed.[13]

Paton may have been a pioneer in location, but not in methodology. He was the antithesis of avant-garde. He attempted to establish churches with the three-self characteristics—self-governing, self-supporting, and self-propagating—though

---

[12] Mission Synod Minutes, pp. 192-93, cited in Barnes, *Aneityum*, pp. 101-02.
[13] F. Paton, *Kingdom in the Pacific*, p. 138.

admittedly this methodology was probably in its infant stages. Over the period of many years and upon the anvil of much suffering, Paton developed this model and made it the centre of his missionary practice.[14] Graham Miller says the indigenous principles of the Aniwan church were such that they sent out their own converts as evangelists to other islands and 'elected its elders and a pastor, Kamasiteia, the first in the history of the mission'.[15]

From the beginning the missionaries knew westerners would never win the South Seas for Christ. They would have to teach and disciple the natives. It is not surprising then that Paton never refers to himself in his *Autobiography* as a *pastor*. His chief aim was the establishment of indigenous churches. He was a missionary, a fact the church must never forget. 'Our object in sending out missionaries is not to form new branches of our own church, but to plant and develop a strong native church that will ultimately be self-supporting, self-governing, and self-propagating.'[16]

He was careful not to imitate those missionaries that 'cease to be movable evangelists and become pastors'.[17] He was there

---

[14] And he no doubt passed this on to his son, who wrote: 'The [missionary's] whole aim is to build up a strong, self-supporting, self-propagating, and, as far as possible, self-governing native church. Through his teachers he multiplies himself a hundredfold, and the work spreads further and further afield.'

[15] Miller, 'Paton, John Gibson', *Australian Dictionary of Evangelical Biography*.

[16] F. Paton, *Kingdom in the Pacific*, p. 76.

[17] Roland Allen, *Missionary Methods: St Paul's or Ours?* (Grand Rapids: Eerdmans, 1962), p. 57. Allen said elsewhere, 'The conviction that new converts can beget new converts leads them from strength to strength: the conviction that they will fall if they are not nursed leads them from weakness to weakness.' *The Spontaneous Expansion of the Church* (Grand Rapids: Eerdmans, 1973), p. 34.

to stay, but with the goal to leave. 'Humanly speaking, there is no other way in which these tribes and peoples can be evangelized. The next state will be that of the native pastorate, with a very few superintending European missionaries—a stage on which, for instance, my own Aniwa has long since practically entered, the elders carrying on all the work for the church, with an occasional visit from a neighbouring missionary. But the foundations of the civilization and of Christianity must either be laid and solidly built up by a missionary for each of these peoples, or they will never be laid out at all.'[18]

A cup of cold water

Prosperity hucksters were active even during Paton's day. One Roman Catholic renegade swindled money from churches by forging credentials and claiming to be Paton's alternate in the New Hebrides. Straight from the health and wealth playbook, the man even promised to etch the names of big donors upon the bronze sheeting of the ship.

Just like today, clear thinking about finances was essential. Paton's philosophy about money and missions can be hung upon three hooks: generous giving, self-supporting churches, and humble fund-raising.

First, Paton was liberal in charity toward the islanders. When he determined to dig a well because of the scarcity of good drinking water[19] he was met with great resistance

[18] Paton, *Autobiography*, p. 495.
[19] Their island's drinking water came either from a boiling hot spring or from rain collected during the wet season. Fresh water was needed mostly for cooking, as the

from the natives because they had never heard of such a thing. They thought the tropical sun had driven him mad. 'Everyone knows water comes from the sky, not the ground. The people will never believe your message if you go forward with such foolishness.'

Though the people refused to take part in the foolhardy task, the crowds gathered to watch as Paton dug metre after metre alone. The chief set a relay team of men to watch over him because he was certain the missionary was digging his own grave before suicide. 'Thus I toiled on from day to day', Paton later wrote. 'My heart almost sinking sometimes with the sinking of the well.' Then the water came. 'Muddy though it was, I eagerly tasted it, lapping it with my trembling hand, and then I almost fell upon my knees in that muddy bottom as my heart burst up in praise to the Lord. It was water! It was fresh water.'[20] What a torrent of wonder and awe followed! Though Paton was an evangelist through and through and disinclined to proffer social aid without much thought, he would later say that it was the sinking of the well that broke the back of heathenism on Aniwa. It won such a pervasive hearing that the gospel spread through the entire island. The chief, who had trampled under foot Paton's teaching, was now seen brandishing his tomahawk in church, swinging it

---

natives bathed in the ocean and quenched their thirst by drinking coconut milk. As for washing clothes, their wardrobe was minuscule!

[20] Humorously, after becoming accustomed to the somewhat brackish water on the island, he confided to have sprinkled a little salt into his tea when first tasting fresh water from Australia!

enthusiastically behind the pulpit as he urged the people to believe in Christ and abandon their idols.

Second, Paton was adamant the native church should be self-supporting as soon as possible.

> In all my work amongst the natives, I have striven to train them to be self-supporting, and have never helped them where I could train them to help themselves. In this respect I was exceedingly careful, when the question arose of building their churches and schools.[21]

The church buildings of the natives were modest, constructed by the congregation, and did not cost the churches back home a single penny. All of this was by design. Despite the native Christians' lack of means, they learned to give and work and save without foreign aid alleviating their responsibilities.

> The greater part of the work is, apart from the salaries of the foreign workers, self-supporting. They pay for their own Scriptures, build their own churches and schools, largely support their own teachers and preachers, and in many other ways help to lighten the financial burden of the work. In addition to this, thousands of pounds are contributed annually to the funds of the various Foreign Mission Boards.[22]

Did the first Bible translation reach the islands through charity? Hardly. It came through over a decade of consecrated toil, the natives using their cash crop of arrowroot to pay for

[21] Paton, *Autobiography*, p. 363.
[22] F. Paton, *Kingdom in the Pacific*, p. 105.

the publishing of Scripture, the *Westminster Shorter Catechism*, and even portions of Bunyan's *Pilgrim's Progress*. As missionaries translated, 'the willing hands and feet of the natives kept toiling through fifteen long but unwearying years, planting and preparing arrowroot to pay the £1,200 required to be laid out in the printing and publishing of the book'. Paton then adds a sound rebuke for the church: 'Let those who lightly esteem their Bibles think on those things. Eight shillings for every leaf, or the labour and proceeds of fifteen years for the Bible entire, did not appear to these poor converted savages too much to pay for that word of God.'[23]

With the modern mission fields bloated with foreign assistance and cross-cultural donations, why did these missionaries of old insist the native church bear the expenses of the local pastors and other church needs? Because though the sacrifice and toil would be great, 'nothing other than good could come of such a strong incentive to labour. It would help to solve the many problems that rise from the natural tendency to indolence on the part of the people. All this would lead to a deeper feeling of responsibility, and would provide a spur to spiritual endeavour.'[24]

Third, the amount of time Paton spent fund-raising would surprise most people. He was able to discern that his idyllic dreams of remaining on the front lines of island missions was not the wisest use of his time and gifts. Michelsen expands: 'As Dr Paton's fame as a mission lecturer has gone long before

[23] Paton, *Autobiography*, p. 78.
[24] F. Paton, *Kingdom in the Pacific*, p. 139.

these pages, and will go where this short account will never reach, it is needless for me to add that it was judged that his time would be better spent moving about interesting the churches in the New Hebrides mission than to remain on Aniwa among a small and decreasing population.'[25]

In these early days of missions in the South Seas the greatest challenge was just getting to the field. After the arduous journey to the nearest departure point for the New Hebrides (usually Australia), the missionary would wait patiently for a vessel, then often leapfrog from boat to boat until he finally arrived at his station of labour.

To overcome this problem, the various missionary societies began building up their fleets of ships. With such an urgent need to transport the missionaries, Paton was called upon to travel throughout Australia and Europe to raise funds. Though he urged people to give generously to God's work, personally, he was notoriously frugal. He was ever meticulous with missionary funds, on some occasions sleeping in the open air rather than hurt the mission budget with hotel fare. On another occurrence, he took a train to a meeting but was mistakenly given a seat in first class. 'I want third, please', he said. 'I'm a missionary from the South Seas, and missionaries never travel first class.' Though miserly in meeting his own needs, Paton was generous in giving away most of the royalties he earned from the *Autobiography*, transferring hundreds of pounds to fund hospitals, training colleges, and translation work on the islands.

---

[25] Michelsen, *Cannibals Won for Christ*, pp. 176-77.

Paton's simple method of raising funds was remarkable both by today's standards and his own. He never overtly solicited funds from individuals in general or the wealthy specifically, but made a broad appeal to the churches of the needs of the New Hebrides. Contrary to modern missionary methods, where most gifts are sent directly to the mission board, most of the money was sent to him directly, to which he kept meticulous records, sent the giver a note of receipt, and then passed it on to the mission himself. This is even more extraordinary because many of the gifts were small in nature—not large subscriptions but ordinary shillings and pence of the masses—meaning ample more paperwork. Nor did he overreach in fund-raising platitudes suggesting God had 'promised' a certain amount. He was content. 'If [God] does not so send it, then I shall expect he will send me grace to be reconciled to the disappointment, and I shall go back to my work without the ship.'

He was also a pleader. Despite his physical weakness, his love for the islands transformed him such that the audience hung on his every word. 'As a pleader,' his son said, 'he had no equal.' One preacher in Glasgow knew this and when encouraging his people to give generously to the mission, he added that they should only bring the amount of money they intended to give that evening, 'else you will return home leaving all in the collecting plate'!

Graham Miller believes one of the secrets to Paton's impact on islanders and abroad was that he never forgot a face or a name.[26] And then, of course, there is something to be said for

---

[26] Miller, 'Paton, John Gibson', *Australian Dictionary of Evangelical Biography*.

time-tested measures such as getting on one knee and looking a youngster in the eye. Paton may have had the boldness of a lion, but he also had the heart of a child. This made people want to give. On one occasion, while Paton was raising funds for the mission, a little girl sat upon his knee—exclaiming with confidence that she had his picture and had known him for some time. The elder missionary, with long white whiskers streaming down his face, was puzzled. Then she exclaimed: 'You are Moses! Only you haven't got the tables of stone in your hands now!'

God used Paton's grit, cheery personality, and tireless work ethic in a mighty way. The money poured in far beyond anyone's expectations. Later when the mission ship approached Aniwa, Paton's son, though just a boy at the time, recalls in vivid detail the sense of excitement the welcome sight generated: '[I] well remember the intense excitement on the little sea-girt island of Aniwa when the white sails of the *Dayspring* appeared upon the horizon just twice a year. The grown-ups thought of letters from loved ones far away, but the youngsters thought of biscuits without weevils, mission boxes, and just possibly a tin of lollies to be doled out at the rate of one a day as long as the tin lasted, and they often wished that Elijah would come along and make it last out like the widow's barrel of meal!'[27]

Social reform

Today's Insider Movement—that softens the differences between Islam and Christianity by allowing minimal change

---

[27] F. Paton, *Kingdom in the Pacific*, p. 58.

in converts—would have appalled Paton. He preached the past *and* present aspects of salvation and expected the same kind of all-encompassing life-change the apostle Paul did, who implored his converts to turn to God from idols (1 Thess. 1:9). Contrary to some modern missionary strategies urging a free salvation without a sin renunciation, the apostle Paul did not gloss over the pagan beliefs of his native audience. He implored 'converts from a pagan background to abandon important parts of their heritage and to give up central convictions and patterns of behaviour of their culture'.[28]

Paton's holy boldness in denouncing the social sins of his day is most clearly seen in the matter of the Kanaka Labour Traffic. The unspeakable suffering of this slavery movement was built upon the backs of the South Sea islanders. In the nineteenth century, 'kanaka' (Hawaiian for 'man') referred to a South Sea native indentured to labour in the sugar and cotton plantations of Australia. In time, however, it was a reference to a South Sea slave. So disgraceful were these methods that the practice ended in 1863 due in part to protests by the British government. When it was revived in 1892 (albeit with heavy restrictions), Paton and the other missionaries stood in strict opposition to it. He wrote to the Premier of Queensland, Australia: 'I do most earnestly plead with you, in the interests of humanity and for your own honour and the honour of Australia, not to renew this Polynesian labour traffic.'

Paton spoke out about a host of other social sins committed by both whites and blacks. His stand against the

[28] Schnabel, *Paul the Missionary*, p. 359.

common practice of wife beating was unwavering—as were his protests against infanticide and widow-burning; in the case of the latter, women were often saved from the pyre at the eleventh hour. In a letter to her husband dated June, 1894, Margaret Paton gives a glimpse of the poor conditions the native women faced:

> [On the custom of removing a woman's front teeth] I hardly know [the women] from the men until they smile. … The want of two upper front teeth proclaim them to be the weaker vessels—slaves to a horrid custom which still prevails, and I suppose will prevail till Christianity has got a firm hold.

> [On one of the three murders during her stay] The victim was a poor native woman who had been a long time sick. Her husband got tired of the bother of keeping her, so they buried her alive!

> [On the price for women who flee their husbands]: The awful practice is to put a red-hot stone under a woman's knee and tie back the leg to keep it there till the stone grows cold. No running away after that—a woman is lamed for life![29]

He called the matter of multiple wives a 'delicate issue' but refused to allow practising polygamists into church membership. On one occasion he watched a chief at his baptism give up eleven wives, all of whom were later remarried, the chief remaining a devout Christian until the end.[30]

---

[29] Langridge and Paton, *Later Years and Farewell*, pp. 83-86.
[30] Geddie records the marriage of four polygamists who, 'in obedience to the dictates of Christianity, had given up the practice. After a public declaration that

The matter of alcohol split the missionaries[31] but when it came to racism—that sin which nineteenth-century Europe loved to coddle—Paton unloaded his sentiments with both barrels:

> It would give a wonderful shock, I suppose, to many namby-pamby Christians to whom the title 'Mighty to Save' conveys no ideas of reality, to be told that nine or ten converted murderers were partaking with them the Holy Communion of Jesus! But the Lord who reads the heart, and weighs every motive and circumstance, has perhaps much more reason to be shocked by the presence of some of themselves.[32]

---

they renounced all claims on the women with whom they had parted, they were regularly married to those whom they chose to retain as their wives.' Patterson, *Missionary Life Among the Cannibals*, p. 367.

[31] Some missionaries believed kava-drinking should exclude a Christian from communion. Peter Milne, a missionary from Scotland, refused to co-operate with any missionary or native teacher who smoked or drank. Surprisingly, Inglis and Paton—both avowed teetotallers—voted against the motion to exclude alcohol drinkers from membership.

[32] Paton, *Autobiography*, p. 335.

10

Paton's Relentless Evangelism

What think ye of this, ye scoffers at missions? What think ye of this, ye sceptics as to the reality of conversion? He died, as he had lived since Jesus came to his heart—without a fear as to death, with an ever-brightening assurance as to salvation and glory through the blood of the Lamb of God, that blood which had cleansed him from all his sins, and had delivered him from their power. I lost, in losing him, one of my best friends and most courageous helpers; but I knew that day, and I know now, that there is one soul at least from Tanna to sing the glories of Jesus in heaven—and oh, the rapture when I meet him there![1]

—John G. Paton

PATON'S first wife and child died before the boxes were unpacked in their new island home. They had been on Tanna for less than three months, beaming with hope that the cannibals would one day be converted. Paton's wife was still in her teens—his only child but six weeks.

[1] Paton, *Autobiography*, p. 160.

Sovereignty as fuel, not foe

In the wake of this unimaginable sorrow, nearby missionaries assembled on the island to pass a resolution. Was it a pact for greater protection? Was it a pledge to greater vigilance over physical health and safety? In part it was. Most notably, however, it was a commitment to a greater focus on evangelism. They wrote: 'Regard this striking dispensation of God's providence as a loud call … to be more … diligent in pressing the concerns of eternity on the minds of others.'

From what fabric is such dogged evangelism woven? From where comes such concern for the lost and such determination to win them? From the unshakable truth of the rule of God over all things, including the seeking, softening, and saving of sinners. Does God's sovereignty over salvation kill missionary zeal? For this consecrated crew of South Seas missionaries, the thought was preposterous.

John Paton was a firm believer in the doctrines of grace. He stands as one soldier in a long line of godly missionaries who assailed the foreign field armed with the resolve to 'endure everything for the sake of the elect' (2 Tim. 2:10).

Scripture teaches that God's sovereign grace fuels the fervour of missions. Since the book of Acts is the most evangelistic and missions-minded book in the Bible, we would expect to find this truth throughout. And in fact, we do.

Three strong texts

In Acts 18:10 the risen Lord said to Paul, 'I have many in this city who are my people.' After a rough go of it in Corinth, Paul may have been having thoughts of moving on. But the Lord came to him in a dream, urging him to 'go on speaking and do not be silent' (18:9). The Lord then gives a three-part motivation for evangelism: his presence ('I am with you'), his protection ('no one will harm you'), and his promise ('I have many in this city who are my people').

The promise, of course, is that there were people in Corinth who are his 'other sheep' whom he must bring into the fold and who will listen to his voice (John 10:16). They have been chosen. By virtue of this, even though they have yet to believe, Jesus already considers them his.

But does this really *fuel* evangelism? It did for Paul. Corinth was the first city where Paul settled for an extensive period of missionary service; he stayed there for a year and a half. He did not respond by saying, 'Since God has his people, I guess I'm not needed here.' Rather than being a deterrent to missions and evangelism, election was the incentive that kept Paul to the task when times got tough.

In Acts 16:14 we are told: 'The Lord opened [Lydia's] heart to pay attention to what was said by Paul.' God is always the initiator in salvation. He is the founder of our faith (Heb. 12:2). The engine of God's grace gave Lydia the willingness to learn ('the Lord opened her heart'), which in turn pulled the caboose of Paul's evangelism ('attention to what was said by Paul').

That which sustained Paton through years of evangelism was the reality that God *will* save his people. How often on those dusty paths did pain of rejection bid him quit? How many times had the impenetrable human heart forced this missionary's hands up in despair? But—he no doubt remembered—it is God who opens hearts. 'Regeneration', Paton would write, 'is the sole work of the Holy Spirit in the human heart and soul.'[2]

The life raft of sovereign grace upon the sprawling ocean of evangelism is Acts 13:48: 'As many as were appointed to eternal life believed.' In the previous verse, the Gentiles bring salvation to the ends of the earth (13:47). In the following verse, the gospel is spreading through the entire region (13:49). Luke's words in between make it work. Acts 13:48 is the hub that makes the wheel of evangelism turn.

Luke reminds us that Christians are elected to believe, not because they believe. Those who believe do so because God determined it (Eph. 1:4). But God's inscrutable plans do not negate man's responsibility. Thus, elsewhere, Paul could guarantee the hands on deck, 'there will be no loss of life' (Acts 27:22), yet balance it with the warning 'unless these men stay in the ship, you cannot be saved' (27:31). God saves through the means of evangelism.

These truths sustained Paton when evangelism was near impossible. In his early days on Tanna he faced a common missionary conundrum—men too embarrassed to study

[2] *Ibid.*, p. 372.

Scripture alongside their wives. At night the male leaders would slink Nicodemus-like into Paton's home to learn 'the Worship' when they were assured all the blinds were drawn. They could not grasp the cost of discipleship, with one chief admitting: 'I would be an Awfuaki man (i.e. a Christian) were it not that all the rest would laugh at me; that I could not stand!' But this did not dampen Paton's gospel resolve, for he knew the moment Jesus took the reins of their hearts, they would happily believe.

Casting the net

Paton spoke the way consistent Calvinists should. 'My heart bleeds for the heathen, and I long to see a teacher for every tribe and a missionary for every island of the New Hebrides. The hope still burns that I may witness it; and then I could gladly rest.'[3]

His work of teaching the gospel never stopped. On Sundays catechism classes and a prayer meeting followed two morning sermons. The afternoon was given to hut-to-hut discipleship. Paton knew that while regeneration is the work of God evangelism is the task he has given men to do. The reward that comes from such consecrated duty is immeasurable.

> Life, any life, would be well spent, under any conceivable conditions in bringing one human soul to know and love and serve God and his Son, and thereby securing for yourself

at least one temple where your name and memory would be held for ever and for ever in affectionate praise—a regenerated heart in heaven. That fame will prove immortal, when all the poems and monuments and pyramids of earth have gone to dust.[4]

He criticized the armchair sceptics who evangelized the world from the comfort of their own home. Like the Jews who were astounded the Spirit should rest upon the Gentiles (Acts 10:45), many of Paton's contemporaries wondered if such a lack of civility could grasp such a glorious message. Were these pagans really converted? 'All [their] doubts would dissolve under one glance of the new light that Jesus, and Jesus alone, pours from the converted cannibal's eye.'

One must not think, however, that Paton's protracted efforts in evangelism were merely cerebral; compassionate teaching most accurately describes his method, as can be seen in the following example. Nerwa, a chief on Aniwa and a keen debater, reasoned that because Paton had never seen God with his eyes nor heard him with his ears, he must therefore not exist. And he threatened to run the missionary through with a spear if he insisted he did. Let the reader here be reminded that dexterity in apologetics is necessary among all peoples, including the lesser cultures of the world, for Paton claimed the agnostics of the islands could reason their case just as well as any European.

Paton, however, did not rebut his native counterpart with logic and exegetical arguments. Instead, he kept quiet and let

[4] *Ibid.*, p. 413.

his actions speak. When the Patons showed compassion to the orphans and taught them children's songs in the Aniwan tongue, the icy hearts began to thaw. Mothers soon were converted, then fathers, and finally Nerwa, who eventually lived long enough to be an elder and spiritual leader of the church. Love is the universal language.

Revivalism back home

While Paton was labouring in the South Pacific, a new philosophy of ministry was taking root in Western Europe. Entering churches on both sides of the Atlantic was a kind of decisionistic evangelism which soft-pedalled the importance of doctrine and conviction of sin. Instead, it focused on assaulting the emotions usually through anecdotal preaching and the appeal or invitation system.

In the 1870s Paton was seeing many conversions on Aniwa. Though Charles G. Finney died in 1875, his evangelistic method of adapting means to secure impressive 'results' was still very much alive. At this time, D. L. Moody and Ira D. Sankey—on the heels of their New York Revival—were bringing a form of revivalism to Scotland rarely seen before. From November 1873 to March 1874, the Great Revival moved through Edinburgh—some considered it to be the greatest revival movement in Europe since the days of John Wesley's preaching in England. Others, however, had their doubts.

Moody himself *did* preach repentance. He also shunned listing as converts those who asked for prayer after a service, a move that won the support of Spurgeon and Andrew Bonar. Still, there were enough threads of revivalism woven not only throughout the Revival movement but also through a number of Scottish churches that caused considerable concern. In London, Spurgeon vocally opposed those who immediately published the number of converts or announced a 'revival' before the fruit was visible. 'I am weary of the public braggings, the counting of unhatched chickens, this exhibition of doubtful spoils.'[5]

Think of the temptation Paton faced to mimic such methods, especially when some donors back home expected to hear of instant results. If Paton faced the push for quick conversions several generations ago, how much more the missionaries and evangelists of the contemporary church! J. I. Packer conveys what happens when we fail to trust in God's sovereignty:

> We are tempted to be in a great hurry with those whom we would win to Christ, and then, when we see no immediate response in them, to become impatient and downcast, and then to lose interest in them, and feel that it is useless to spend more time on them.[6]

Paton never succumbed to such erroneous ways of thinking. His evangelism never lacked a call to repentance, and

[5] Iain H. Murray, *Revival and Revivalism: The Making and Marring of American Evangelicalism 1750-1858* (Edinburgh: Banner of Truth Trust, 1994), p. 408.

[6] J. I. Packer, *Evangelism and the Sovereignty of God* (Downers Grove, IL: IVP, 1991), p. 119. For another excellent resource on the doctrines of grace with an evangelistic spirit, see Steven J. Lawson, *Foundations of Grace* (Lake Mary: Reformation Trust, 2006).

this in spite of the hostility such a call provoked. The gospel message must focus its attack precisely where the defences are strongest:

> When we began to teach them that, in order to serve this Almighty and living Jehovah God, they must cast aside all their idols and leave off every heathen custom and vice, they rose in anger and cruelty against us, they persecuted every one that was friendly to the mission.[7]

But Paton did not avoid supplying numbers altogether. If Luke could speak of 3,000 being saved on the day of Pentecost, Paton certainly had warrant to provide statistical evidence of God's grace. And yet he was aware of the dangers ulterior motives might play in counting 'conversions'. Take note how the following quotation reflects the teaching of the Parable of the Soils (Mark 4):

> On our own Aneityum, 3,500 cannibals have been led to renounce their heathenism. On our New Hebrides, more than 12,000 cannibals have been brought to sit at the feet of Christ, though I mean not to say that they are all model Christians. And 133 of the natives have been trained and sent forth as teachers and preachers of the gospel.[8]

First, he gave these numbers in retrospect; that is, he gave the 'converts' time to show their identity as true believers. Second, he also notes that not all Christians look the same. Some had merely left heathenism but were not 'converted' in

[7] Paton, *Autobiography*, p. 74.
[8] *Ibid.*, p. 265.

the biblical sense. Some went forth as preachers ('a hundred fold'), some were not 'model Christians' ('thirty fold'), but all converts bore fruit in some shape or form. Third, though Paton was never one for numbers, he nonetheless rejoiced over the sheer volume of converts on the other islands and was unafraid to recount them. Paul the missionary never gave statistics but Luke the missionary historian did—though mostly in round numbers to communicate such data is valuable but not *that* valuable.

Paton: a model of dogged evangelism

Paton's belief in a sovereign God, coupled with his resolve to win the natives to Christ no matter the cost, no matter the sacrifice, no matter the loss, and no matter the penalty, is in the end what brought a whole island to faith.

This blessed blend of doing the work and dependence on God is a good reminder to those of all vocations and callings. Parents should remember that while teaching children the gospel, the message must always dwell beneath the banner: 'Salvation belongs to the Lord' (Jon. 2:9). Laymen must keep in mind that the perfect illustration that will help a co-worker understand the gospel better is not *the thing* that will ultimately save them. Missionaries must not crumble when the locals cackle at the accent in which they speak. They may shun and scoff and spit and stew, but this will never negate the promise that God will unlock the hearts of sinners just as he did with Lydia. God's sovereignty does not kill missionary vigour. It assures victory and guarantees success.

The sweet synthesis of divine election and tenacious evangelism kindled the wonder of the natives:

> We slew or drove them all away! We plundered their houses and robbed them. Had we been so treated, nothing would have made us return. But they came back … to tell us of their Jehovah God and of his Son Jesus. If their God makes them do all that, we may well worship him too.[9]

The murderer of Canadian missionary George Gordon, and his child.

[9] *Ibid.*, p. 310.

APPENDIX A

Timeline

1773 Captain James Cook explores the New Hebrides

1824 Born May 24, near Dumfries, Scotland

1839 John Williams is martyred on Erromanga

1848 John Geddie begins first effective work on Aneityum

1852 John and Jessie Inglis arrive in Aneityum

1858 Marries Mary Robson; arrives on Tanna later that year

1859 Wife (19 years old) and infant son (36 days old) die three months after arrival

1861 George and Ellen Gordon are martyred on Erromanga; Samuel Johnston dies after 7 months on Tanna

1862 John and Mary Mathieson die; Paton escapes Tanna for Australia

1864 Marries Margaret Whitecross; *Dayspring I* arrives in New Hebrides; Patons reach Sydney on 27 December

1865 First child Robert is born

1866 Returns to the New Hebrides; settles on Aniwa

1867 Fred Paton is born

1870 Third son, Frank, is born on Aniwa

1872 John Geddie retires; dies

1873 *Dayspring I* is wrecked; Lena Paton born; dies 6 days later. Leaves for 6 months to Australia

1874 Returns to Aniwa; Synod insists Paton must return to Australia after six months to recover but decides to stay on Aniwa

1880 Margaret gravely ill; Walter Paton dies aged 30 months

1881 Leaves Aniwa with family

1884 Commissioned to raise funds for a steam ship; leaves Aniwa for the UK

1886 Begins six years of travels in Australia raising funds for the New Hebrides

1889 Visits Aniwa after eight-year absence; *Autobiography* published

1892 Begins his trip 'round the world for Jesus'; Fred goes to Malekula

1893 Writes from New York: 'Not losing a moment of time'

1894 Leaves New York for the UK; meanwhile, Margaret visits Fred in Malekula; her *Letters and Sketches* published

1895 Sails to Tanna on behalf of son; *Dayspring 3* launched

1896 Frank begins six-year ministry on Tanna; *Dayspring 3* wrecked after fourth voyage

1897 New Testament in the Aniwan language published; last revision of *Autobiography*

1899 Around the world aged 76

1900 Fred marries in Melbourne

1901 Leaves the UK; reaches Melbourne July 31, having travelled 44,000 miles

1902 Sails to the islands with Margaret; catechism and hymnbook published in Aniwan

1903 Leaves Aniwa

1904 At 80 years old, visits Aniwa for the last time; visits sons Fred and Frank on the islands

1905 Margaret dies at age 64

1906 Refused by the Committee to return to the islands; brother James dies on December 27

1907 Dies on January 28 at the age of 82

1910 *Later Years and Farewell* published by A. K. Langridge and Frank Paton

APPENDIX B

Paton's Family Tree

John G. Paton's grandchildren.

The family tree below illustrates how four generations of the Paton family served the New Hebrides Church, 1858-1970:

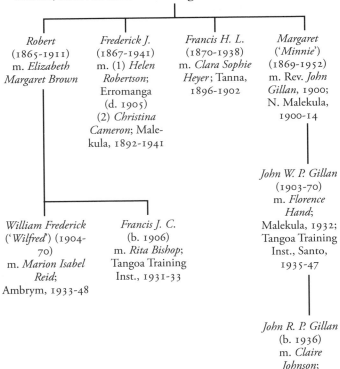

Dr *John G. Paton* (1824-1907), Tanna, 1858
First wife, *Mary Ann Robson*, married 1858,
died with infant son *Peter Robert Robson*, Tanna, 1859
Aniwa, 1866. Second wife *Margaret Whitecross*, Aniwa.

Robert
(1865-1911)
m. *Elizabeth Margaret Brown*

Frederick J.
(1867-1941)
m. (1) *Helen Robertson*;
Erromanga
(d. 1905)
(2) *Christina Cameron*; Malekula, 1892-1941

Francis H. L.
(1870-1938)
m. *Clara Sophie Heyer*; Tanna, 1896-1902

Margaret
('*Minnie*')
(1869-1952)
m. Rev. *John Gillan*, 1900;
N. Malekula, 1900-14

John W. P. Gillan
(1903-70)
m. *Florence Hand*;
Malekula, 1932;
Tangoa Training Inst., Santo, 1935-47

William Frederick
('*Wilfred*') (1904-70)
m. *Marion Isabel Reid*;
Ambrym, 1933-48

Francis J. C.
(b. 1906)
m. *Rita Bishop*;
Tangoa Training Inst., 1931-33

John R. P. Gillan
(b. 1936)
m. *Claire Johnson*;
Malekula and South Santo, 1955-70

APPENDIX C

A Poetic Tribute

All Nations Sing for Joy [1]
A Missions Anthem in Honour of John Paton

All nations sing for joy,
each tribe and tongue and kingdom;
like clouds infused with rain,
pour all your praise upon Him.
The gospel now unfurled,
glad servants He shall send
to every land and realm,
and then shall come the end.

All churches fast and pray,
the Spirit bids you, sending
an army full of hope,
a multitude unending.
Adorn the hills with praise,
with feet arrayed in truth,
proclaim the treasure hid,
and gates of hell subdued.

[1] May be sung to the tune of *Nun Danket* ('Now Thank We All Our God').

All martyrs to be slain,
your blood at Satan's bidding;
lift high the Victor's hymn,
for Jesus goes on winning.
God's sheep held in contempt,
the world intent to kill;
the same your Lord endured,
now His afflictions fill.

All choristers confess
Jesus the Lamb unblemished;
unsullied blood once shed
for sinners that would perish.
This psalm of thanks a ray,
His work of grace the sun;
for now and evermore,
the song has just begun.

—Paul Schlehlein

APPENDIX D

A Defence of Paton's Eloquence

THERE is a fine line between biography and hagiography. Since this book relies heavily on the records of the missionaries themselves, it is open to criticism from those who believe first-hand missionary accounts are unreliable due to their alleged hyperbole and elaborate flavouring.[1] Paton was not exempt from such a charge.

While it is true he was a colourful and vivid writer, Paton's critics' charges of embellished or triumphant language are unmerited. There are a number of reasons for this.

First, Paton has biblical precedent for his style of writing, for the Scriptures (at times) emphasize the virtues of its heroes by magnifying their strengths without always elaborating on their weaknesses.

---

[1] In regard to cannibalism specifically, Paul Moon—with no particular proclivity for missionaries—argues that the majority of missionary accounts in the South Seas were in fact correct. 'The revisionists would argue that reports of cannibalism in the eighteenth and nineteenth centuries were frequently made to excite audiences back in Europe—that their creators used the widespread ignorance of many indigenous cultures to conceal their falsifications, and thus were elate to deliver to their readers horridly lurid stories about people eating human flesh … It all seems to make sense, but it is all totally wrong.' Paul Moon, *This Horrid Practice*, p. 30.

Hebrews 11 never mentions the drunkenness of Noah (verse 7), the dishonesty of Abraham (verses 8-9), the unbelief of Sarah (verse 11), the deceit of Jacob (verse 21), the anger of Moses (verses 23-30), or the immorality of Rahab (verse 31). Instead, the text focuses on their heroic acts of faith. The author of Hebrews was not dishonest when neglecting to show the vices of God's saints because his purpose was to encourage faith in the heart of the believers to whom he addressed his brief word of exhortation (Heb. 13:22). Not saying everything that could be said is not the same as speaking erroneously. Missionaries of the past whose writings gravitate toward gospel victories were unashamedly seeking to rouse people's hearts for Great Commission work. In doing so they were following in the footsteps of the inspired penman.

Second, some narratives of danger that may seem to be inflated *only appear that way* because some fields of missionary service *really are* more hazardous than others.

Peter Barnes, who is generally very favourable toward Paton, suggests that while Paton told his story in vibrant hues, John Geddie was an example of one who resisted the urge to exaggerate. 'Geddie was particularly immune to sensationalism and self-dramatisation. He refused to play on the home church's emotions.'[2] Hence, the following quotation from Geddie:

> It is a matter of thankfulness that in all our visitations we
> have not met with the slightest interruption or molestation

[2] Barnes, *Aneityum*, p. 6.

of any kind. On no occasion have we seen or heard anything to awaken our fears as to our personal safety.[3]

This may seem to imply that Paton's accounts of extreme danger were somewhat inflated. But a closer look shows otherwise. We must note that Geddie gave this testimony early in ministry before many of his hardships arose. Moreover, Tanna—where Paton spent his first four years of missionary service—*was* more dangerous and hostile than most of the other islands, especially Aneityum where Geddie ministered. Tanna was even considered too dangerous for the Gordons, who were later martyred on Erromanga. Geddie himself notes that 'Aneityum with all its faults appeared more attractive to me than ever, having seen the degradation and misery of other islands.'[4] In October 1852 some native Christians asked Geddie if they could visit Tanna to re-establish the work there. Cautious Geddie did not immediately encourage it. When Paton later relocated to the precarious, but less dangerous island of Aniwa, he toned down his language.

Third, it is an unfortunate reality of some interpersonal relationships—even at times among missionaries—that envy can colour opinion and cloak reality. It would be understandable, then, if contemporaries and successors of Paton—some of them more experienced than he—would struggle with feelings of resentment as they witnessed Paton's rise to worldwide fame. Geddie, though a man of meek character, sometimes

---

[3] John Geddie, Miscellaneous Papers, 1844–1877, Folder C.
[4] Geddie, *Misi Gete*, p. 133.

appears overly critical of other missionaries. He was unafraid of charging Paton of taking too dour a view of Tanna, Gordon of misplaying his hand on Erromanga, and Inglis of mismanagement on the *Curaçoa*. Conversely, Paton rarely—if ever—criticizes other missionaries in his *Autobiography*. He typically comes to their defence.[5] Since envy, by its very nature, is invisible to human eyes, attempts to prove that it was rooted in criticisms of Paton's language would be nearly impossible. Still, it would be wise for readers to remember that jealousy among successful colleagues is not unheard of (1 Sam. 18:8-9) and is often the source of conflict (James 4:1-2).

Fourth, eloquence isn't the same as grandiloquence. The former is a virtue, the latter a vice. Paton was a gifted writer. While wisdom is preferred to eloquence, if an author can employ both as Paton did, it will make for a delightful read. His editor (his younger brother James) certainly improved his writing, as a good editor should, but this does not mean that James Paton *falsely* coloured his brother's writings. Spurgeon, a master orator in his own right, could have simply referred to Paton as 'a fine leader of threatening Polynesian islanders'. Instead, he referred to him as 'King of the Cannibals'. No wonder the moniker stuck. No wonder Paton's *Autobiography* is still read today.

---

[5] Paton made it known, however, that he was displeased with Geddie's position on the *Curaçoa* affair and the criticism he received because of it. 'God's people are still belied. And the multitude are still as ready as ever to cry, "Crucify! Crucify!"' Paton, *Autobiography*, p. 304.

Fifth, theological positions play a larger role than most people realize when it comes to 'style' of language. Depending on one's interpretation of unfulfilled prophecy, a post-millennialist (usually more optimistic) will sometimes—if not subconsciously—portray events in a more positive light than a pre- or a-millennialist (usually more pessimistic). Therefore, the 'understated' or 'overstated' language may have less to do with pride than with a distinct worldview. So when Saul-sized calamities arise on the mission field (an incident of crime or sickness, for example) one side portrays it Goliath-like and the world stands back in horror. The other side portrays the tragedy David-like and the audience is encouraged by such a small disturbance. Both portrayals are viewed through the lens of their doctrinal worldview.

Finally, no matter what language a missionary uses, he will rarely satisfy all tastes. Should he present the culture and practices of the natives in a negative light, he will be charged with overstatement, discrimination, and bigotry. Should he swoop to their defence, protect them under his wing, and charge their oppressors with malpractice, he will be charged with paternalism. Toning down one's language may alleviate charges from one side, only to increase them from the other.

In sum, John Inglis, a contemporary of Geddie and Paton, states it best when denying the missionary candidates were misled by highly-coloured reports:

> I have no hesitation in affirming that, taken as a whole, the
> reports and letters of the missionaries on this group, in point

of truthfulness and accuracy, and in the absence of all false colouring, will stand a favourable comparison with those of any mission in Christendom.[6]

---

[6] *Reformed Presbyterian Magazine*, January 1869, p. 24, quoted in Barnes, *Aneityum*, p. 5.

Bibliography

Allen, Roland, *Missionary Methods: St Paul's or Ours?* (Grand Rapids: Eerdmans, 1962).

—*The Spontaneous Expansion of the Church* (Grand Rapids: Eerdmans, repr. 1973).

Barnes, Peter, *Aneityum: Missionary Methods and the Theology of Mission* (Wipf and Stock, 2015).

Bavinck, J. H., *An Introduction to the Science of Missions* (Philadelphia: Presbyterian and Reformed Pub. Co., 1960).

Bell, Ralph, *John G. Paton: Apostle to the New Hebrides* (Butler: Highley Press, 1952).

Bonar, Andrew A., *The Letters of Samuel Rutherford* (1891; repr. Edinburgh: Banner of Truth Trust, 2006).

Burton, John Wear, *The Fiji of Today* (London: C. H. Kelly, 1910).

Campbell, John, *The Martyr of Erromanga: Labours, Death, and Character of the Late Rev. John Williams* (London: John Snow, 1842).

Carey, S. Pearce, *William Carey* (1923; repr. London: Wakeman Trust, 2008).

Charnock, Stephen, *Works* (1864; repr. Edinburgh: Banner of Truth Trust, 2010).

Cromarty, Jim, *The King of the Cannibals* (Darlington: Evangelical Press, 1998).

Defoe, Daniel, *Robinson Crusoe* (1719; repr. London: T. Hughes, 1824).

Garretson, James M., *Princeton and Preaching: Archibald Alexander and the Christian Ministry* (Edinburgh: Banner of Truth Trust, 2005).

Geddie, John, *Misi Gete*, ed. by R. S. Miller (Launceston: Presbyterian Church of Tasmania, 1975).

Gutch, John, *Beyond the Reefs: The Life of John Williams, Missionary* (London: Macdonald and Company, 1974).

Gordon, J. D., *The Last Martyrs of Erromanga* (Halifax: MacNab and Shaffer, 1863).

Henry, Matthew, *Matthew Henry's Commentary on the Whole Bible: Complete and Unabridged in One Volume* (Peabody: Hendrickson, 1994).

Howie, John, *The Scots Worthies* (1870; repr. Edinburgh: Banner of Truth Trust, 2001).

Kane, J. Herbert, *Christian Missions in Biblical Perspective* (Grand Rapids: Baker, 1976).

Kirklady, Allen, *Capturing the Soul: The Vhavenda and the Missionaries, 1870–1900* (Meno Park: Protea Book House, 2005).

Klauber, Martin I., and Manetsch, Scott M., *The Great Commission: Evangelicals and the History of World Missions* (Nashville: B & H, 2008).

Kuiper, R. B., *God-Centred Evangelism* (London: Banner of Truth Trust, 1966).

Langridge, A. K., and Paton, Frank, *John G. Paton: Later Years and Farewell* (London: Hodder and Stoughton, 1910).

Larsen, Timothy, Bebbington, David W., Noll, Mark A., *Biographical Dictionary of Evangelicals* (Downers Grove: IVP Academic, 2003).

Lawson, Steven J., *Foundations of Grace* (Lake Mary, FL: Reformation Trust, 2006).

Lovett, Richard, *The History of the London Missionary Society, 1795-1895*, vol. 1. (London: H. Frowde, 1899).

Macleod, John, *Scottish Theology* (Edinburgh: Banner of Truth Trust, 2015).

Melville, Herman, *Moby Dick* (1851; repr. New York: Farrar, Straus, and Giroux, 1997).

Michelsen, Oscar, *Cannibals Won for Christ: A Story of Missionary Perils and Triumph in Tongoa, New Hebrides* (London: Morgan and Scott, 1893).

Miller, J. Graham, *A Day's March Nearer Home* (Edinburgh: Banner of Truth Trust, 2010).

—*Live: A History of Church Planting in the New Hebrides* (Sydney: Committees on Christian Education and Overseas Missions, General Assembly of the Presbyterian Church of Australia, 1978–1990).

—'Paton, John Gibson (1824–1907)', in *Australian Dictionary of Evangelical Biography.*

Moon, Paul, *This Horrid Practice: The Myth and Reality of Traditional Maori Cannibalism* (New York: Penguin Books, 2008).

Murray, Iain H., *A Scottish Christian Heritage* (Edinburgh: Banner of Truth Trust, 2006).

—*Revival and Revivalism: The Making and Marring of American Evangelicalism 1750-1858* (Edinburgh: Banner of Truth Trust, 1994).

—*The Puritan Hope: A Study in Revival and the Interpretation of Prophecy* (London: Banner of Truth Trust, 1971).

Packer, J. I., *Evangelism and the Sovereignty of God* (Downers Grove: IVP, 1991).

Paton, Frank, *Lomai of Lenakel: A Hero of the New Hebrides* (London: Hodder and Stoughton, 1903).

——*The Kingdom in the Pacific* (London: London Missionary Society, 1913).

Paton, John G., *The Autobiography of the Pioneer Missionary to the New Hebrides (Vanuatu)* (1898; repr. Edinburgh: Banner of Truth Trust, 2016).

Paton, Margaret Whitecross, *Letters and Sketches: The New Hebrides* (1894; repr. as *Letters from the South Seas*, Edinburgh: Banner of Truth Trust, 2003).

Patterson, George, *Missionary Life Among the Cannibals: Being the Life of the Rev. John Geddie, D.D., First Missionary to the New Hebrides* (Toronto: James Campbell & Son, James Bain & Son, and Hart & Co., 1882).

Piggin, Stuart, and Roxborogh, John, *The St Andrews Seven* (Edinburgh: Banner of Truth Trust, 1985).

Piper, John, *Brothers, We Are Not Professionals: A Plea to Pastors for Radical Ministry* (Nashville: Broadman & Holman, 2013).

——'George Müller's Strategy for Showing God' (Minneapolis: Desiring God, 2004).

——*John G. Paton: You Will Be Eaten By Cannibals!* (Minneapolis: Desiring God, 2012).

Schmidt, Alvin J., *How Christianity Changed the World* (Grand Rapids: Zondervan, 2004).

Schnabel, Eckhard J., *Paul the Missionary* (Downers Grove: IVP, 2008).

Sproul, R. C., 'What Does the Bible Say About Courage?' Accessed May 10, 2016, www.ligonier.org.

Tucker, Ruth, *From Jerusalem to Irian Jaya* (Grand Rapids: Zondervan, 1983).

Varg, Paul A., 'Motives in Protestant Missions, 1890–1917', *Church History* 23, no. 1 (March 1954): 68-82.

Ward, R., ed., *Presbyterian Leaders in Nineteenth Century Australia* (Melbourne: Aust. Print Group, 1993).

Winter, Ralph D., and Hawthorne, Steven C., *Perspectives on the World Christian Movement: A Reader*, 4th ed. (Pasadena, CA: William Carey Library, 2009).

The Banner of Truth Trust originated in 1957 in London. The founders believed that much of the best literature of historic Christianity had been allowed to fall into oblivion and that, under God, its recovery could well lead not only to a strengthening of the church, but to true revival.

Interdenominational in vision, this publishing work is now international, and our lists include a number of contemporary authors along with classics from the past. The translation of these books into many languages is encouraged.

A monthly magazine, *The Banner of Truth*, is also published. More information about this and all our publications can be found on our website or supplied by either of the offices below.

THE BANNER OF TRUTH TRUST

3 Murrayfield Road,   PO Box 621, Carlisle,
Edinburgh, EH12 6EL,   Pennsylvania 17013,
U.K.   U.S.A.

www.banneroftruth.org